↻ CAN'T GET THERE FROM HERE ↻

a collection of alleged humor writing

JEFF TOMPKINS

Scene33

Copyright © 2010 Jeff Tompkins

All rights reserved.

Except as permitted under the US Copyright Act of 1976, no part of this publication may be reproduced, distributed or transmitted in any form or by any means, or stored in a database or retrieval system, without prior written consent of the Author.

Paperback edition: August 2011
E-book edition: September 2010

ISBN-13: 978-1460947173
ISBN-10: 1460947177

Also by Jeff Tompkins

49 MIX TAPES

a novel

available in paperback and e-book
DECEMBER 2011

CONTENTS

The Modern Dating Scene	1
Humor Theory	5
In Defense of Public Education	9
Mr. Break-it	12
Basebore	16
There Ought to be a Law	19
Turtles, Ghosts and a Side of Bacon	23
Could I Get That in Writing?	31
Customer (Non)-Service	34
Nothing to See Here	38
Keep Your Hands Off My Beans	41
Annual Family Christmas Letter	45
Extra Rice, Please	48
House Hunters	52
Side Effects	58
Take This Song and Shove It	61
The Case Against Summer	64

Warning! Ignore at Your Own Peril	68
Web of Conceit	71
Who Are You Wearing?	75
Cool to be Kind	78
Dig This	82
How Not to Write a How-to Article	86
Nothing More Than Feelings	90
Outta Sight	94
Spelling Beeeezzzz	97
Tale of an Adoring Fan	101
Getting Some Distance	106
Googling Yourself	110
Man vs. Plastic	113
Odd Job	118
Transcript (U.S. Navy Talks to Somali Pirates)	121
We Aren't The Champions	125
These Kids Today	129

But wait! There's more!

How May I Help You Very Much?	133
Must See TV? I'll be the Judge	137
Survival Can be a Bear	140
What's in a Name?	144
Stuff It	147
Talking Small	150
Weather Advisory	153
Twenty	156

THE MODERN DATING SCENE

Relationship experts tell us that dating has never been easy, and in fact may be more complicated now than ever. I have never seen the data so I'm assuming they're telling the truth, but it seems to me that dating has always been complex.

Take, for example, the Caveman Era. At the time there were no restaurants and movie theaters, so there was the problem of coming up with something to do on a date. But they didn't even have language, just grunting. Therefore, the caveman didn't have to be concerned about being "shot down" by the cavewoman because they couldn't even talk. Dating basically consisted of one caveman clubbing another caveman over the head and taking his cavewoman. This process would go on and on, until football was invented, distracting caveman and giving cavewoman a few hours to herself. Many historians believe that while cavemen were grunting and getting crumbs all over their shirts while sitting on the couch watching football, cavewomen were advancing society. But of course the cavemen took all the credit.

So things have always been complicated. Today, however, no one seems to have time to date. And if you're a single adult, it seems that everyone is married, so what's the point in even trying? Where are single people going to find the time and the other single people?

You could try Internet dating sites. These are websites where you specify exactly what you're looking for—height/weight preferences, taste in music and movies, number of functioning limbs, etc.—and then the site matches you up with a serial killer. Not good.

Now where do you go?

TV. That's where.

There have been dating shows almost since the advent of TV, but today's shows are very different from those in the '60s and '70s, and not just in terms of hair size.

The Dating Game, which first aired in 1965, consisted of a main contestant and three potential dating candidates. The candidates were seated behind a partition, out of the view of the main contestant, who would ask them a series of questions like, "Bachelor Number One, if you were stranded on the moon, what kind of food would you want to have with you?" And the suave bachelor would give a suave answer like, "Ice cream, because it's sweet, but not as sweet as you sound!" Of course this makes no sense because, let's face it, if you were stranded on the moon, the only thing you'd be thinking about is avoiding space monsters and suing somebody if you made it back to Earth.

After nearly three seconds of research, I was able to determine that there have been at least thirty dating shows on TV in various formats. Some of them involve monetary conflicts designed to create more suspense.

For example, on the show *For Love or Money*, the main contestant was a female who had to pick, from a group of guys, the one whom she believed to be her best match. But there was a twist. The guys knew that if they were picked, they would have to choose whether to date her or take home a million dollars. And if she picked a guy who picked her instead of the million dollars, she would win two million dollars. So she had to pick the "right guy," which as far as I could tell, she didn't, because like the rest of us, she was confused by the show's format. "Wait, I pick the guy who wants the million dollars or wants me or the one who wants to give me a million dollars or what?!" was a common phrase heard during the show.

Another show that involved a money conflict was called: *Who Wants to Marry a Multi-Millionaire?* I never saw this show, but I do know the answer: almost everyone who doesn't currently have multi-millions themselves.

The most interesting of these shows was called *Average Joe*. I'm not proud of this, but I watched it. Laugh if you must, but I did it so you wouldn't have to. The female contestant was presented with a group of (you guessed it!) "average Joes," ranging from overweight truck-drivers to 96-pound nerds who probably grew up wishing they could marry Princess Leia from Star Wars, or, if she wasn't available, perhaps C3PO.

The twist on this show was not money, but rather a group of infiltrators called "hunks." Toward the end of the show, they brought in guys who were not "average Joe" truck-drivers and nerds; they were the type of guys who appear to work out even when they're asleep, and also have never read anything more complicated than a STOP sign. As you might have guessed, the average Joes were not pleased. How were these unfit laborers and pimple-flecked video-gamers supposed to compete against guys who could crush an aircraft carrier with their abs? I mean, aside from clubbing them over the head like the cavemen did.

The answer, of course, is that they couldn't. But for some reason the girl ended up selecting one of the Average Joes anyway. I'm still not entirely sure why, but it had something to do with the fact that he was able to express his feelings for her through the written word. Or he had a million dollars, I forget which.

The dating scene isn't so bleak. There are single people out there. Sometimes the guy does get the girl, even if she seems out of reach. All we single people need now is our own TV show. Failing that, we're going to have to go back to doing it like the cavemen did, and where do you find a big wooden club these days?

~~~

HUMOR THEORY

One of the oldest questions in human civilization (other than "Who was the first person to eat an egg, and why?") is: "What makes something funny?"

Dictionaries offer many definitions of humor, one of them being: "The four fluids of the body: blood, phlegm, choler, and black bile." But that's not the kind of humor we are talking about here.

The humor we are talking about here is defined by my dictionary as: "the tendency of particular cognitive experiences to provoke laughter and provide amusement." This is not very helpful to the average person looking for a clear meaning, because the average person has no idea what "cognitive" means. Most of your average people won't even use a dictionary. I think a better definition, something that could be understood by all, is "anything that causes you to involuntarily make a sound like 'ha ha.'" Everybody can relate to that.

But perhaps the best answer is: We don't really know what humor is. Humor is subjective. Different people find different things funny. For instance, some people think Larry the Cable Guy, Ron White and Jeff Foxworthy are funny, while other people don't. It's a matter of preference, and clearly the first group's preference is wrong.

Humor appears in many forms: satire, parody, jokes, pranks, political promises, people falling down, etc. The first joke occurred in 3257 B.C., when a caveman picked up a rock and, in caveman grunt-language, said, "Get a load of this rock." But the rock turned out to be a dried lump of dinosaur dung. The other cavemen in the area laughed and wished that video cameras were already invented so they could send in a clip to *America's Funniest Videos*.

Satire and parody are attempts at mocking or ridiculing their objects by exaggerating certain aspects of the object. Often the purpose of satire goes beyond amusing the audience; its chief aim is to make a point by using wit and sarcasm. This is best done when the object is a person, a group of persons, or an institution that holds power or claims knowledge beyond the understanding of the simple-minded, everyday schmo such as you. So it's fine to satirize CEOs, politicians and meteorologists (who love sending me emails correcting my highly scientific columns on weather), whereas it would be mean-spirited to make fun of those who have no power or knowledge, such as celebrities, unless you can think of something really funny, and then it's OK, so forget this rule.

Pranks or practical jokes are also vehicles for humor. An example of a decent prank is gluing someone's mailbox shut. An example of an even better prank is making an anonymous phone call to a person and telling them that their mailbox has been glued shut, but when they go out to the mailbox, they find that it is *not* glued shut, and they open it and instead find out that you put a Black Mamba snake in there. If you're going to put such a deadly snake in a mailbox, you should take the proper precaution to avoid a disastrous outcome for yourself. Placing an item in a mailbox without a stamp is a federal offense, so you should put a stamp on the snake, preferably on the tail.

Humor is something that can magically appear out of nowhere, such as a witty remark during a conversation, or it can take a while to develop, especially in longer forms such as books, movies and even newspaper columns. For example, the version of this column you're reading right now is the 142nd draft, and was started in 1987.

Sometimes you can make something funny simply by changing a word or two. For instance, the phrase "That politician is a jerk" is not very funny. The phrase "That politician is a conniving crapmonkey" is a little funnier. But the phrase that would elicit the most laughter from your audience would be "That politician is an ethical person who is looking out for the average person."

Humor is complicated and not something that can be easily defined. You can't take humor and place it in a small box covered with fancy black velvet. To do so would be to reduce the value of humor to something completely worthless like a diamond. Humor is an even more precious gem, a rare find, something that can be found in microscopic traces during a Dane Cook performance.

To sum up: If at any point during your reading of this, you smiled, laughed, chuckled, guffawed, LOL'd, giggled, hooted, chortled, snickered, cackled or made a sound resembling "ha ha" (even in your mind) then you found something humorous here. If, however, you did none of those things and found yourself thinking "This isn't funny at all," I will be glad to give you a full refund. Send me your address and I'll call you and tell you when to check your mailbox....

~~~

IN DEFENSE OF PUBLIC EDUCATION

Another poll has been released showing that Americans are stupid. These come out every few years, exposing us as a people who don't know the most basic aspects of history, science, math, etc. (The "etc." is listed because sometimes people don't even know what subjects they know nothing about.)

The point of these research polls is, I guess, to shed light on our dysfunctional education system. That, or simply to uncover new and exciting ways to make jokes about average Americans: "You expect people to understand the tax code? They can't even locate the United States on a map!" (It's right next to the ocean.)

I'm a product of public education. I remember having to memorize the states and their respective capitals. Sure, I can't remember all of them *now*, but I don't need to know them now. I only needed to know them for the test. And even then, I only needed to memorize about thirty of them because the other twenty fit nicely on a small cheat sheet. I also remember having to learn the Pythagorean Theorem. That's a mathematical formula by which you can find out how long one side of a triangle is. Or two sides. I can't remember. What I do know is that I have never had to use this in real life. My geometry teacher told the class that it was helpful for figuring out things like how tall a flag pole is. I don't remember what she said after that because I was sitting there trying to figure out why I'd ever need to know how tall a flag pole is. Maybe if I went to work for a flag pole company or something, but you'd think they'd just put a label on the box.

There was also an obsession among history teachers about dates. What year did Ferdinand Magellan discover America? What year did the colonies declare independence from New England? When did Abraham Lincoln deliver the famous line: "The only thing we have to fear is fear itself"? What year did Lee Harvey Oswald walk on the moon? Stuff like that.

That Americans can't answer these questions is no great indictment of our intelligence. It just proves that we discard superfluous information. There are, however, some basic things that we all remember, because they're important.

For instance, we all know that our first president, Benjamin Franklin, chopped down a cherry tree as part of a series of experiments that led to the invention of the telephone.

We also all know that it takes the sun one month to revolve around the earth. However, during a leap year (which happens when the groundhog sees his shadow) the opposite happens, and the earth revolves around the sun. This takes about one leap year.

The vast majority of Americans will tell you that they're good at basic math, which is all that's important. As I stated earlier, there is no need for any type of "theorem" in real life. The same is true for the "cosine" and the "square root," both of which probably don't even exist outside of math class. We are told that all that complicated math is necessary for things like space exploration and medical research, but most of us don't go into those fields. Most of us need just enough math to know that if you go into a store with a twenty-dollar bill and purchase something that comes to $12.68, you should get back roughly three dollars. That's all you need to know, really. Being able to make change is probably the most important aspect of your daily life. If you don't believe me, listen to some speeches by the remaining presidential candidates. They are constantly talking about making change.

Spelling, grammar and vocabulary, however, is both important. You don't need no dictionary or nothing to learn how to talk good. You just need to read and pay attention to what you reading, and I ain't talking about no classic writers neither. Just smart people who write good.

Public education lately has come under fire for emphasizing standardized tests to the detriment of the subjects that would constitute a well-rounded education, like music, theater and the other arts. I think the criticism is unjustified. Today's kids know plenty about music, probably more than those of us who went to school a decade or more ago. How else can you explain the fact that the average ten year-old can download a gigabyte of music before you can even figure out how to turn on your iPod? See? They're fine.

To be sure, there is one depressing aspect of our education system and that is the failure to teach people the fine art of critical thinking, which I'm sure will be evident when this paper receives letters from people complaining about all the misinformation in this article.

~~~

MR. BREAK-IT

Right now you're probably sitting around thinking: Is there anything worse than finding out that your air conditioner isn't working in the middle of winter? Of course there is. Why would you even ask? But while we're on the subject, I might as well go ahead and tell you that I discovered, just after Christmas, that my AC wasn't working. I guess it's better that I find out at this time of the year, rather than in the summer when, here in Charleston, SC, the temperature often approaches 170 degrees. And that's the *low*.

I would have tried to fix it myself, but I'm not familiar with heating and cooling units. Plus, I'm not even sure where it is. Or, for that matter, *what* it is. The only thing I'm familiar with is the thermostat. I decide what setting to put it on by moving a little lever or switch or something, then there's a clicking noise and the air gets warmer or cooler. Being mechanically disadvantaged, I have no idea how this works, but I'm going with magic because it's a concept that is easier to grasp.

Anyway, I called the guy to come fix it. This is a guy who I have personally witnessed repairing complicated things such as the back of a broken refrigerator using only a pair of tweezers and a quarter-inch snippet of electrical tape. And if you have ever taken a long look at the back of a refrigerator, you know how complex those things are and also you were looking at the wrong side because the door is on the front. Another time the stove wasn't working and he fixed it using a different method, which he explained to me like this: "It came unplugged. I plugged it back in for you."

My point is that this guy is very good at what he does. So I was relieved when he showed up carrying a toolbox the size of a Volkswagen Beetle, containing more tools than they probably have in the entire U.S. Navy fleet. He's not a very big guy, but he carried that toolbox with great confidence. I get the feeling he probably takes it with him to bars to impress the ladies. Whatever works.

It was a good thing that he brought all those tools because the only one I have in my house is a mellon-baller and I'm not even sure why it's here. I may also have part of an old hammer, but I can't be too sure. That's the kind of "Mr. Fix-it" guy I am.

He started working on the unit and, as I sat far away, I could hear him talking out loud to himself. At least I hope he was talking to himself because he was using technical terms, only one of which I recognized. "The compressor seems OK," he said, and I was still with him at that point because I know that a compressor basically compresses things. But then he started using other phrases, none of which I had any clue about, such as: "Your sequencer got stuck."

I didn't ask him what it meant that my sequencer got stuck; I just said, "Ah-ha," as though I was in the loop as to why the unit had broken, but of course I had no idea what he was talking about. He could have said, "The disgrontificator has submergified into the haldronic fubble," and I would have responded the same way. He looked at me for a second and then turned his attention back to his work, probably thinking, "Did he just say 'Ah-ha'? I remember this guy now. He called me to plug his stove back in."

After about an hour of work, he had disassembled and reassembled a large portion of the heating and cooling machine (is it even a "machine"?) but it still wouldn't work correctly. In addition to not putting out cool air, it had started producing popcorn.

No, actually it had also stopped putting out hot air. The situation was getting worse, but he remained calm, making confidence-inspiring remarks like the two following verbatim quotes that I swear are true: "COME ON, DANGIT!" and "I'm going to KILL this thing!"

I didn't respond to these outbursts. I just sat there grimacing sympathetically, so that if he turned around again he wouldn't see me laughing and decide to disassemble *me*. (Incidentally, I tried to make it appear as though I wasn't paying attention to the mishap-in-progress, when actually what I was doing was making notes for this column.)

He did finally get it working again, both the AC and the heat, though I have no idea what he did. I could live to be 5,000 years old and I still wouldn't understand it. Nor do I really care. All I know is that when he got it working, the last step was to test the temperature of the air coming out of the...whatever-they're-called. I call them "air things." He did this by using something that looked like a gun with a small screen on it that displayed the air temperature, which is picked up by—get this—a real-life laser. And you thought I was kidding about this guy's toolbox.

I was glad to have the thing fixed and I'm thinking that we should send this guy to repair the International Space Station. I have no idea what's wrong with it, of course, but I'm sure if I had been up there I would have been the one who broke it. Or, more likely, forgot to plug it in.

~~~

BASEBORE

Lately I've been doing something I don't normally do: watching baseball. The sport is just too slow, much slower than my favorite sport, football. But I've been watching recently because the NCAA tournament is underway, wending its way through regional and "super regional" match-ups in college towns across the country. (It also helps that my favorite team is still in the tournament. When they're out, so am I.)

This is the only time I can sit through an entire baseball game—when the games actually seem to mean something. That's even more the case in the pros, where they play 162 regular season games, which means, theoretically, that a team could lose forty or fifty games in a row and still make it to the World Series. There's no urgency to any single game until you get to the end of the regular season.

My relationship with baseball started, as it does with most American boys, when I played little league. My main contribution to the team was the ability to get a critical strike-out just when it really mattered. Unfortunately, I did that as a batter and not a pitcher. And I did it often.

My rare appearances on base were due almost exclusively to being walked. The only time I remember making contact with the ball and getting it in fair territory was the time I got hit in the head with a pitch and the ball fell just in front of home plate.

I wasn't much better at fielding. I was not an aggressive player, so naturally the coach always stuck me out in right field, that being the place the ball was least likely to go if someone got a hit. I spent a great deal of time out there trying to stay away from bees.

That was also perhaps the most religious period of my life, because I put a great deal of effort into praying that no one would ever hit the ball to me. If I were to dig deep enough into my psyche, I could also probably find a link between that time and my lifelong interest in meteorology, because I used to stand out in right field scanning the skies, hoping that the clouds would gather themselves into a thunderstorm and mercifully bring an early end to the game.

Not that I'm bitter or anything! Honest. My inability to get excited about a baseball game really has more to do with the game itself, which someone once described as "one minute of action spread over three hours."

I realize that there are good reasons for the slow pace of the game: players need time to kick dirt and spit; coaches need time to sprint out onto the field and argue with umpires about whether a guy was safe or out ("He was out!" "No he wasn't!" "Yes he was!" "No he wasn't!") and whether a pitch was a ball or strike ("That was a strike!" "No it wasn't!" "Yes it was!" "No it wasn't!"). I get that. But couldn't we still have those important aspects of baseball and tweak the rules just a bit, in order to speed this thing up and make it a little more exciting?

I have come up with a few suggestions that I believe would greatly improve the game of baseball.

First, I would add a pitch clock, much like the play clock in football and the shot clock in basketball. If the pitcher fails to get into his wind-up within the allotted time (let's say 25 seconds) it counts as a ball. This would prevent delays in the game caused by pitchers looking around the stadium, wandering around the mound and looking down at the dirt as though they're on a beach looking for shells. Enough of that.

The next rule change I would make is to allow a batter to choose whether he runs to first or third after getting a hit. This would create a little suspense for the fielders and of course the viewers. The only restriction would be that once you start going in one direction (counter-clockwise or clockwise) around the bases, you have to keep going in that direction. You can't get a hit, run to third and then, on the next play, run home. Too easy.

This means we would probably have to adjust the rules to allow multiple runners on the same base at the same time. Even better. Then we'd have play-by-play announcers saying things like, "The count stands at two balls, two strikes, and we've got two men on first and three on second, no outs." You can't beat that for excitement. Or confusion.

My last suggestion—and this may seem contradictory because it could potentially remove some of the excitement from the game—is to do something about those bees out in right field.

~~~

THERE OUGHT TO BE A LAW

Several years ago a friend of mine overreacted to something I said and called me a "fascist." What I had said was that I thought it should be illegal for man to date a woman who is taller than he is. Talk about the breakdown of civil discourse in our politics! There I was, trying to offer a practical idea that would greatly improve the future of our society and all he could do was fire back with something that is all too common these days in political discussions: unprovoked name-calling and personal attacks. There's an old saying that goes something like this: Name-calling is the last refuge of an exhausted mind, you brainless jackass!

We continued to be friends and he continued to call me names when I would come up with additional policy recommendations. For instance, when I suggested that people should be subjected to fines and/or imprisonment for using the phrases "no ifs, ands or buts" and "any way, shape, or form" or say that someone is "not a happy camper," he again accused me of being a fascist.

OK, maybe he was right.

Over the years he modified his label for me. No longer was I simply a fascist; because of the allegedly impulsive, reactionary and arbitrary nature of my political ideas he started calling me a "whimsical fascist." The label stuck because, well, I guess because I would often begin the presentation of my views with something like, "If I ever become Dictator of the United States," followed by a proposal for a new law that would be along the lines of the aforementioned thoughtful and sensible initiatives.

So I suppose it's not completely unjustified to call me a "whimsical fascist," but don't we all have a tyrannical streak in us? Everyone, at some point, has observed something annoying and declared: "There ought to be a law." You know you have. You know everyone has; even candidates for public office who, I should remind you, have the actual power to put something into law. But they always let us down. They're always coming up with things like minimum wage increases, military spending, safe drinking water standards and education funding. They never tackle the difficult stuff. (Aside from declaring National Ferret Appreciation Month.)

So here are a few suggestions of things for which people should be prosecuted:

People who lick their fingers before turning pages and *especially* when they're counting money that they're about to hand to us. Why don't you cut out the middleman and go ahead and just spit directly on us? Extra jail time should be attached for those who are found guilty of doing this during cold and flu season.

People who seem a little too enthusiastic about how I'm doing, especially if they say, "Doin' okay today?" *Today*? Why don't you care how I was yesterday, or how I will be tomorrow? And don't you know that the question "How's it going?" or any variation of it, is really just another way to say hello? No one *really* wants to know how anyone else is doing, particularly in a cashier/customer setting. Just move it along.

People who ask "Hot enough for ya?" Just assume that, yes, it is hot enough for me and I'm about to burst into flames and take you down with me.

People who drive at half the posted speed limit. Especially the people who seem to be coasting all the way to their destination. If they tell you they're going to the store and you ask which one, they respond, "Depends which way the wind is blowing."

People who use credit cards for everything. If you go into a gas station and purchase Tic-Tacs with your credit card, something is wrong with you.

People who whistle in public. No one else wants to hear the noises you're creating with your mouth. Has everyone noticed that these offenders are never whistling actual songs or even semi-coherent melodies? It's as though they're walking around the grocery store composing an original piece. (A piece of *what*, I won't say, but most of you know what I'm talking about.)

People who know they're going to write a check and don't even have their checkbook out by the time the cashier has scanned all of their items. And if you're one of those people who write checks very sloooowwwly, as if you're in a handwriting contest, you shouldn't be eligible for parole.

You're probably thinking: *Whoa! I'll have to remember not to vote for this guy if he ever runs for office!* Guess what? If I ever become dictator of the United States, everyone who reads my columns will be ineligible to vote. Unfortunately, that might be the only idea of mine that will ever be taken seriously by politicians.

~~~

TURTLES, GHOSTS AND A SIDE OF BACON

Years ago, I was an avid viewer of *The X-Files*. If you're not familiar with the fictional series, it was basically about two people who investigate paranormal phenomena. If you did watch the series, you know it as the show that featured one of TV's greatest mysteries: How many years can a group of television writers drag out a story arc before the viewers start egging their houses and demanding to know what the hell is going on?

Like many people, I gave up on the show after a few seasons, so I was surprised to hear good things about last year's movie, *X-Files: I Want To Believe*. I plan to watch the movie this Friday, but in the meantime I started to wonder about the people who take the paranormal seriously.

Why, exactly, do they believe in this stuff? Do they have proof? Do they even *want* proof? These are questions that a serious journalist working on a feature article would ask. Therefore, it was my duty to take a completely different approach.

I didn't want to talk to anyone on the phone and I wasn't seeking an in-depth face to face interview, but I did want to find out what happens if these people receive ridiculous and sarcastic questions. That's just one of the great things about the Information Age: you can conduct investigative journalism entirely on the Internet without leaving your desk. Nor do you have to go to a parking garage in the middle of the night to meet a shadowy figure named after a 1970s porn film. Eat your hearts out, Woodward and Bernstein.

One of the first strange things I found was an ad for a service that offers "turtle removal." This isn't what you'd call "paranormal," but it was odd enough and I had to start somewhere. I wanted to talk to this person, not because I have any unwanted turtles—I don't have any *wanted* turtles, for that matter—but rather because, well…who wouldn't want to talk to someone who makes a living removing turtles?

I sent this: "I am having some problems with a particular turtle. I have a small pond out back and this turtle has completely taken over. The ducks left and the fish are swimming around terrified. I worry about them. I have tried several methods of getting him out of there, such as small firecrackers placed strategically around the edge of the lake but he just doesn't seem to care. I think if I gave him a lighter he would light the fuses himself and laugh (if turtles laugh). I have no idea what kind of turtle this is, but it is extremely arrogant and rude. Please let me know if you might be able to help with this. Thank you."

Whoever is in charge of the customer service department at this turtle removal outfit is very prompt, because within about twenty minutes I received this: "It's probably a big snapper. I can set out a trap if you would like."

How cold, I thought. No concern about my having tried to take out the turtle with explosives, and no compassion expressed for the frightened fish. Further, this person was obviously not surprised about the reptile being arrogant and rude, which really says a lot: this must be widespread throughout the turtle society.

I wrote back: "What happens if you catch it? I don't want the turtle to get hurt, even though he is a jerk, so you aren't going to shoot it or anything are you? I also forgot to mention that I have seen a smaller one around. Could be his wife."

The turtle guy wrote back: "I don't kill any of the animals. I 'relocate' them."

Something tells me there are a lot of Jimmy Hoffa-type legends in the local turtle community.

I ended it there, seeing as how I don't have a turtle problem and I needed to get on with finding people who are paranormal enthusiasts.

One of the popular touristy things to do in my area (Charleston, S.C.) is to go on one of its many ghost tours, where you pay them a sum of money and they drag you around the city showing you things that don't exist. It's a great business model, and someone should look into whether Bernie Madoff is behind it.

I have never been on one of those tours, nor would I ever pay to go on one, but I'm intrigued by the idea of checking out the mysterious. I sent the following to three different tour companies: "Is there anything to really be afraid of? Have any people seen real ghosts on your tours? I'm interested in taking a tour but I sometimes have an involuntary bodily function response to fear. I will spare you the details, but I just need to know what to wear in terms of protecting my clothing and anything I might sit on. Thanks for any info."

In short time I received the first response, which included this: "A lot of people do find our tours very spooky. Nothing pops out at you or grabs you on any tour, however we cannot predict tour guide behavior."

Forget ghosts—if a business tells you that they cannot predict the behavior of their employees, that's enough to keep me away. Though I'm sure the usual behavior of their guides can't be any worse than the incontinence implied in my email. At least I hope not.

The next day I received a response from another tour group: "Yes, you could get scared! No one jumps out and goes BOO or anything as such. I don't think you have anything to worry about. The tour consists of good stories."

A response from the third company said, quite bluntly: "All of our tours are walking, so you would not be sitting on anything."

And they'd probably make me walk at the back of the group.

Clearly this wasn't going anywhere. They weren't going to answer the question of whether I would see an actual ghost and, with the exception of the third response, no one was going to take the bait about someone ruining a previously good pair of pants. These people are pretty much just in the entertainment business.

In order to find the weirdness, the people who would actually discuss the possibility of the existence of ghosts, I would have to contact the true believers.

I found an organization that bills itself as investigators of the paranormal. This isn't a tour group. These people actually believe in ghosts.

I wrote to them: "I live in a very old house that is rumored to have once been the vacation home of John C. Calhoun, a pro-slavery politician from South Carolina who was a Senator and later, Vice-President. The previous resident told me some strange things go on here, but I thought he was playing it up a bit, in an effort to make the house more interesting. However, since living here, I have not been able to watch B.E.T., *The Cosby Show*, *Fresh Prince of Bel-Air*, and other classic African-American television shows. Even though I have cable, these channels will often not pick up these types of shows. Is there any possibility that a ghost/spirit could interfere with this? I know this might be a question for my cable company, but frankly, I am hesitant about trying to explain this to them. Knowing the cable company, they'd probably try to upgrade me to their 'Ghost-Free Tier' or something. I figured your organization would be more open-minded about this kind of thing, as you've probably seen and heard much stranger stories."

This response came the next day: "I don't believe ghosts or spirits care what we watch on tv. If you are serious we can investigate but something tells me you are putting me on."

A few days later I sent this to another paranormal investigation group: "I came across your site while searching for ghost investigators. Have you ever had any cases where you concluded that a ghost was haunting a car? The reason I ask is that I have amassed what I would call a fairly stunning number of parking tickets (totaling around two thousand bucks) and I don't want to pay them. I am going to hire an attorney but I'd like to have some expert witnesses on my defense team who would be willing to testify that my car is in fact haunted. Even though I come across as someone who doesn't pay for things, I promise I will pay you for your creativity on the witness stand."

They wrote back: "I have heard of haunted vehicles but we are not in the business of taking money for perjury."

I responded: "Does that mean you'll do it for free?"

They didn't write back.

Perhaps I would have to conclude that people in this field, people who are ostensibly more inclined to believe the preposterous, weren't so open-minded after all. Or maybe it's that I wasn't giving them enough credit and they possess more skepticism than I had thought. Maybe they're so good at what they do that they're able to immediately spot a hoax.

Well, maybe some of them. But not all.

I decided to try once more, and found another group, to which I sent the following: "I know this is going to sound strange, but I guess in your line of work you've heard some strange things, so I'm pretty comfortable asking you. I live in an old house (built in 1906) and I am constantly hearing voices, usually in the morning and (here is the strange part) I swear it sounds like they are saying 'bacon.' It could be 'beacon' but it's more of an 'a' sound than an 'e' sound, so I'm wondering....since this happens in the morning, could it have something to do with breakfast? Could this be the spirit of someone who really liked bacon? If you have any kind of sound recording devices, perhaps you could pick this up and analyze it. I have stopped buying bacon because I don't want to taunt the spirit if that is indeed what's going on here. Thanks for any info you can give me."

A short time later, I received their response: "We've heard many strange things before, so this kind of experience is nothing new to us. We haven't had any situations with potential spirits expressing themselves in response to food, but then again, after what we've captured on audio recorders, anything is possible. I think the best way to get some answers would be to have us conduct an investigation for you."

Obviously, nothing in my initial email was too weird for them, so I wrote back: "Do you think it's safe to go ahead and start eating bacon again? I'm just not sure if there could be any danger in doing so (other than long-term health problems, or if some bacon grease gets on the floor and I slip on it)."

They responded, again asking me if I wanted them to investigate, and also: "I would surmise that it's safe to continue eating bacon. Is there anything else going on other than the audio events?"

Me: "Not that I've noticed. Pretty much just the ordering of bacon. I had an idea earlier. I think I might fry some up and leave it out overnight, then see if it's gone in the morning. I don't know if a ghost would eat bacon, but I figure if that's what they want, they'd find a way."

Them: "If you feel like that might get some answers, go ahead and leave some bacon out."

They again offered to investigate, but I had already learned what I needed to know: I have way too much time on my hands.

~~~

COULD I GET THAT IN WRITING?

Recently I have been interacting with a very large organization which I will not name here because they are in possession of many guns and bombs. Granted, most of those items are currently located on a different continent, being used against non-Americans, but I'm not taking any chances.

Anyway, I've been corresponding with them, sometimes by phone but mostly by mail. They mail me far more stuff than I mail them, and if I were to guess the ratio, I'd put it somewhere in the range of 5,000 to 1.

If there's one thing this organization loves, even more than guns and bombs, it's paper. Despite the so-called Information Age, where electronic communication is supposed to be replacing the Era of Paper, this organization seems to be heading in the exact opposite direction, and will soon probably be communicating via ancient sketches drawn on cave walls. And then they'll mail the wall to me.

I guess I was wrong when I figured that most people had made the move to communicating exclusively through electronic means. That's what the Internet was supposed to do. We were supposed to get important information, including forms to fill out, right off the Internet, in the comfort of our homes. We were supposed to get fewer useless items in our old-fashioned physical mailboxes.

It was even said once, by a guy with very thick glasses and many pens in his shirt pocket, that the mailbox outside your house would become obsolete and you'd forget about it. I hoped that would become the case, but I remained skeptical and never believed it. I just couldn't picture people wandering around their yards, unable to locate their mailboxes.

Whatever the case, let's just say I was counting on getting fewer pieces of mail. And not only because of the Internet. I was counting on it because, when I began this fun-filled process, I was notified that this organization was complying with something they call the "Paperwork Reduction Policy." My reaction was: Great! I'll get less mail.

I should have known something was wrong, though, considering all the clues….

When they wrote to me (clue #1, right there) to tell me that they were complying with their own "Paperwork Reduction Policy," the notification was on paper (clue #2), and—you're going to think I'm making up clue #3 but I'm really not, I swear—this "paperwork reduction" notification was five pages long.

But I remained hopeful that the process would go smoothly, with as little paperwork as possible. I would have been better off being hopeful about my prospects of winning the World Series, even though I have not technically set foot on a baseball diamond in roughly twenty-five years, and I am also, as we speak, not currently on the roster of any Major League Baseball team.

Rather than reducing the paperwork, the "Paperwork Reduction Policy" seems to have had the opposite effect. Here's a typical week's worth of mail from The Organization:

On Monday, I'll get a piece of mail telling me I might want to consider, say, Option A. On Tuesday, I'll get a piece of mail that is unrelated to Monday's mail, and seemingly unrelated to anything else that I can figure out. On Wednesday, I'll get a piece of mail consisting of many pieces of paper, and weighing as much as a newborn baby, that goes into great detail explaining Option A that was mentioned in Monday's piece of mail and suggesting, in bold letters, that I strongly consider going with Option A. On Thursday, I'll get no mail. (Have they forgotten about me?)

On Friday, I'll get a piece of mail telling me, in bold letters: "OPTION A DOES NOT APPLY TO YOU. PLEASE DISREGARD OPTION A AND ANY CORRESPONDENCE ABOUT OPTION A."

The only things it does not tell me are: a) why they told me about Option A in the first place, and b) that I should step slowly away from Option A and come out of the house with my hands up. Though I'm sure there's a good chance they'll put that in next Monday's mail because that would give them the opportunity to send me several more pieces of paper, making them even more compliant with their own Paperwork Reduction Policy.

Not that I'm complaining! I have nothing but the highest respect for this organization, if for no other reason than the fact that they have so many guns and bombs.

~~~

CUSTOMER (NON)-SERVICE

I'm sure we all have warm memories of the day when it was possible to call a company and an actual member of the human species would answer the phone by saying, "Thank you for calling [company name]. How may I direct your call?" That day is history. In fact, I just checked the Bureau of Labor Statistics webpage and that day was Wednesday, September 27, 1995.

In the era of automation, where nearly everything is done by computer or some other electronic device, even phone calls are answered by machines. All of this is to ensure that you, the consumer, receive more efficient customer service. Right?

Wrong. Precious hours of our lives that could be spent doing something useful are instead wasted as we navigate our way through corporations' labyrinthine automated telephonic customer "service" systems. The calls usually go something like this:

Press 1 if you are an existing customer. Press 2 if you would like to receive information on our products and services. Thank you. You selected 1. If this is correct, please press 2.

Thank you. Press 1 for customer support. Press 2 for billing questions. Press 3 to return to the previous menu. Thank you. This call may be recorded for quality control purposes.

Press 1 if your product is not working. Press 2 if your product is working.

You selected 1. If this is correct, press 5. Thank you. Press 1 if your product has never worked. Press 2 if your product worked until yesterday around dinnertime.

You selected 1. If this is correct, please press the pound key. Thank you. We here at [company name] are committed to delivering the fastest and most customer-friendly service. Please hold.

(Three minutes of soft piano music...)

Press 1 if your product is still not working. Press 2 if your product started working during the soft piano music.

I'm sorry. I did not recognize that entry. Please try again. Press 1 if your product is still not working. Press 2....

Thank you. Please hold while we connect your call.

(More piano music, plus several enthusiastic advertisements for some of the company's other "fine products"...)

Press 1 if you have your product's serial number. Press 2 if you do not.

You indicated that you do not have your product's serial number. If this is correct, press 1. Thank you. Since you do not have your product's serial number, please locate it and press 2 when ready.

Thank you. For security purposes, please confirm your account by entering the last four digits of your Social Security number, followed by the star key. Thank you. For verification of the confirmation of your account, please multiply 113 by 216 and enter the answer on your keypad. Thank you.

Do you have more than one phone in your house? If yes, press 1. If no, press 2. If you are not sure, ask a family member or roommate, then press 5.

You indicate that you have more than one phone in your house. If this is correct, press 1. Thank you. Please switch to the other phone and press 7 while holding down numbers 3, 8 and 9 while balancing on your left foot.

Thank you. The next available representative will be with you shortly.

(Eleven minutes of soft piano music, with soft saxophone accompaniment...)

If you are still there, press 1. If not, press 2.

You indicated that you are still holding. If this is correct, please use your telephone keypad to enter your approximate weight. Thank you.

If your product is plugged in, press 1. If not, please plug it in and press 2. Thank you. We appreciate your patience.

If you like asparagus, press 8.

Thank you.

If your product is still under warranty, press 1. If not, press 2 or any other number on your keypad because 1 is the only number that would indicate that your product is still under warranty and that's all we really need to know.

You indicated that your product is still under warranty. If this is correct, press 2 three times. Press 8. Press 2 again. Press 1. Press the star key.

Thank you. Please hold while we connect you to the warranty department.

Thank you for contacting the warranty department. Our office is closed. Please call back during regular business hours.

Click!

~~~

JEFF TOMPKINS

NOTHING TO SEE HERE

Today I was going to write about what the new health care plan means for you, but as I was making some notes I realized that I frankly do not care what it means for you. So I had to decide on a new topic, an endeavor that turned out to be more difficult than I thought.

I spent a few minutes considering the idea of writing something about all the celebrity deaths this summer and how our major media has missed the opportunity to dub it "The Summer of Celebrity Death." I don't know what's stopping them. Several years ago they had the "Summer of the Shark" (complete with flamboyant graphics and chilling intro music) and the next year they declared "The Summer of Kidnappings." What are they waiting for?

It can't be that they're waiting for a major pop-star to die, because we just had that. I am of course talking about Gidget, the Taco Bell Chihuahua, who died the other day at age 15. In any case, all the celebrity talk has been overblown, so I chose not to write a single word about it.

Next, I briefly considered writing about the controversy going on in Great Britain over sausage ads.

The company, Mattesons, recently ran some radio spots that included the following: "Think about all the things you can stick this tasty, extraordinarily large sausage in. Mmm... Pizza, pasta, stir fry. You have any ideas? Give me a call and tell me where you like to stick it."

I had a few ideas for that subject, but then the parent company, Kerry Foods, released a statement claiming that the ads were not meant to be offensive, they were meant to be tongue-in-cheek. When I read that, I realized there wasn't much I could say to enhance the comedic value of the story.

Having scratched that idea off the list, I moved on to another recent Associated Press story from Huoma, Louisiana, about a family who is stunned over the fact that a 19-year-old avocado tree is (get ready) producing avocados. Turns out they planted it in 1990 and this is the first time they have seen an avocado on it.

This is a very exciting story, complete with actual quotes from a real-life horticultural expert! I meant to start forming some opinions on this, but failed to do so because, while intently studying the scientific quotes, I fell asleep and later woke up with my cheek in a puddle of drool. Fascinating stories will do that to you sometimes.

For a few minutes I was convinced that I should write about Joe Windscheffel, a defensive back/linebacker who plays for Division-2 Pittsburg State. I wasn't going to write about the missing "h" in "Pittsburg" because we're talking about Pittsburg, Kansas (not Pittsburgh, PA), and there's a state law mandating that colleges may not contain the letter "h" in their names. I'm kidding, of course (though admittedly I haven't checked on it). I was going to write about Joe Windscheffel because he was attacked by a zebra. In case you're wondering, the answer is: No, zebras do not naturally roam the Kansas countryside. Windscheffel was trying to paint a pasture fence and, as is often the case when painting a fence, he had to get the zebras out of the way. A male zebra bit his arm, breaking it, and Windscheffel will not be able to play for the team this year.

I decided not to write about this because it would be too obvious to make a joke about a referee here. The only original and interesting thing I could add would be to point out that the Pittsburg State mascot is "Gus the Gorilla." Again, in case you're wondering, the answer is: No, gorillas do not occur naturally in Kansas. Though I'm sure Windscheffel is not taking any chances and will be on the lookout from now on.

At one point I was sure I was going to write about the old adage: Never rob a Russian hairdresser. Recently, in a town called Meshchovsk (don't try to pronounce it), a would-be robber tried to hold up a hairdresser named Olga who ended up using some karate moves to disarm the guy and tie him up using a hair-dryer cord.

That would be embarrassing enough for the man, but Olga, who apparently doesn't put up with anything from anybody, kept the guy in a storage room, force-fed him Viagra and had sex with him…for four days. You're hoping the humiliation ends there, but it doesn't. When Olga released him, he had to go to the hospital to be treated for (guys, prepare to cringe) torn genitals.

Obviously, that is *not* the type of thing I wanted to write about, and I bet you're glad I decided not to mention it at all. You're welcome.

So, basically, this is just an announcement to let readers know that I don't have anything to write about at this time. Sorry!

~~~

KEEP YOUR HANDS OFF MY BEANS

If you're ever in a certain grocery store in Mount Pleasant, walking down the bread aisle, and you see a container of cooked green beans jammed between two loaves of Wonder Bread, it was me! I put them there.

At this point you're probably thinking I wrote that last paragraph under the influence of an experimental psychiatric drug, but let me explain.

A few months ago, having decided that I wanted a prepared side dish with the chicken I was planning to cook, I went to a grocery store which shall remain nameless so I don't get sued by the time I'm done writing this. I thought the deli would be a good place to pick up some cooked green beans. I was wrong.

Everything went fine during the ordering process. And that is worth mentioning, because placing an order is not always easy, especially if you have to talk through one of those devices at a drive-through that make it sound as if you're ordering from someone who is currently on the moon. Thank goodness the deli wasn't a drive-through, or things could have been much worse than they were. The deli employee began to spoon the beans into a container. One stubborn bean decided that rather than go into the container like all the other compliant beans, it preferred to stay outside, halfway hanging over the rim of the container. Rather than use the spoon that he *already had in his hand*, the deli employee elected to use his ungloved finger to flip the bean into the container.

For a second or two, I couldn't believe what I was watching. Then I remembered that in our current society, even something as seemingly simple and harmless as ordering food is likely to spiral out of control and into a disastrous situation. I didn't say anything to the guy. I simply took the container and walked away. A few minutes later I decided there was no way I was going to buy those beans. I decided to do what any reasonable person would do under these circumstances. Talk to the manager, right? No! I started scouting the aisles for the best place to leave the beans. This turned out to be the bread aisle, as it was the only one that was free of other customers. (You have to be stealthy with things like that.) Then I finished my shopping, paid for the other food I had picked out that had not been directly touched by strangers, and left.

A few weeks later, the same thing happened *again*. Same deli guy. Another order of beans. Same barehanded touching of the beans. It was an astonishing development. Once again, I said nothing, this time because I was beyond being baffled by the repeat offense. I was wondering such things as: What if I hadn't seen him touch the beans and had gone on to eat them, ingesting whatever bacteria this guy walked around with all day? How many people were, at that moment, eating beans that he had touched? Why does he seem compelled to touch the beans!?

So again I found myself searching for a spot to discard yet another container of polluted beans. It seemed my destiny. I was fulfilling some odd new position on the food chain. I didn't go back to that store, for *anything*, for several months. It wasn't because I was afraid of being confronted by management. ("Excuse me, sir, but I'm going to have to ask you to step into the office. We've had reports of someone fitting your description leaving deli containers around the store.") No, I wasn't worried about that. OK, maybe a little. But my primary reason for avoiding the store was that I couldn't bear to look at my arch-nemesis again.

Until…I had no choice. It was lunchtime, I was hungry and in a rush to get to work and that store happened to be the most convenient place to stop. Plus, the other instances had occurred in the evening, so maybe the bean guy wasn't there.

He was. As I came around the corner, heading to the deli with the hope of ordering a *clean* sub, there he was, leaning against the deli case, drumming his bean-seeking fingers on the glass. I decided to wait until he slithered to another part of the deli and someone else moved toward the front; then I would make my move. So I loitered around a nearby cheese display, pretending to regard some of your finer, more snob-oriented cheeses that wouldn't tolerate being stored in the regular deli display case.

A few minutes passed and the Bean Fondler (let's call him "Steve" because that's his actual name) ambled off to another part of the deli. Another guy made his way to the front of the deli. My plan was coming together nicely.

I walked up to the counter and placed my order with the guy. This should have been the end of the ordeal. I had finally defeated the Bean Fondler! Instead, the guy turned toward the back of the deli and shouted, "Hey, Steve! Can you make this guy a sub?"

~~~

ANNUAL FAMILY CHRISTMAS LETTER

It's that time of year again.

Time to send holiday greetings in the form of a letter updating you on all of the boring stuff that you don't care about when it happens during the rest of the year, but that we believe, for some reason, you will find important enough during the hustle and bustle of the holiday season to drop what you're doing and catch up on people you haven't thought about for roughly a year.

First we would like to clear up a misunderstanding. Some of you may have heard back in August that our cousin Sheila was arrested on two counts of breaking and entering. This is not true. The newspapers had it wrong and the lie spread like a fungus. Sheila was actually arrested and charged with just *one* count of breaking and entering. The second count was dropped because there really was no second break-in. See, after gaining entry to the house on the first attempt she accidentally exited the trailer through a door which she thought was a bedroom door but which was in fact the back door, and locked herself out. So she had to break in again. Obviously she is not the sharpest spoon in the drawer.

Jim-Bob no longer wants to go by that name. He says it sounds too country so he is now going by the more sophisticated "James-Bob." He has decided to go back to school after all these years. It's not easy for someone in their 30s to switch to part-time work and put themselves back in a classroom after such a long time. We are very proud of his decision. The guidance counselor tells us that, according to her records, he is the only 11th grader with a full beard. Despite having to take on part-time work, he is making a killing on the weekends buying party refreshments for his classmates. So things are obviously going well, but we are a little nervous about the upcoming prom.

Grandpa is doing fine, but is still upset with us for taking away his car keys. He insists that his mind is functioning well enough for driving, though most of the time he is voicing this opinion to an empty chair or sometimes a wall.

Robert, who has always shown an interest in the legal profession and who has long held the dream of becoming a defense attorney, is getting some "hands on" experience as we speak. Unfortunately, he will be sitting at the defense table in handcuffs. We are sure he is innocent and that there is a perfectly good explanation for his actions. The police seem to think that renting a storage space to house large amounts of Sudafed and lantern fuel is somehow indicative of a meth lab. We believe Robert was simply preparing for the winter, what with his sinus problems and all.

Frank and Edna had to move out of their home after the foreclosure and a brief semi-violent standoff with the Sheriff's Department. Several bad words were yelled by Frank as he toppled off the roof and into a hedge of unkempt bushes. No charges were filed, thanks to the kindness of the Sheriff, who said that considering where some of the branches entered Frank's body, that was punishment enough as far as he was concerned. We were all relieved and got a chuckle out of it. Actually, Frank didn't laugh much.

And lastly, the big news: We are pleased to announce the arrival of a new family member! Sara and her soon-to-be husband Roger added to our ever-growing family this year when they welcomed a baby boy to the world. He is happy, healthy and we are all sure he will lead a full life once the tail is removed. Happy Holidays!

P.S. You may have noticed that this year there are two fruitcakes included in the package. Usually we just send out one per letter, but this year we had some extras. For some reason we received several anonymously sent fruitcakes in the mail this year. It was a nice gesture and we decided to share the generosity with you, the ones we care about most. Enjoy!

~~~

JEFF TOMPKINS

EXTRA RICE, PLEASE

If you've been wondering whether there's anything you should be worried about, wonder no more. I'm here to tell you that you should be worried about a bee chasing a shark that is trying to kidnap someone so it can ransom that person for rice. Confused? Let me explain.

In the summer of 2001, after a series of shark attacks, the cable TV news channels declared that it was the "Summer of the Shark." They reported incessantly about the shark attacks and showed off their impressive graphics and theme music, even though that summer saw thirteen fewer attacks and nine fewer shark-related deaths than the previous year. Similarly, they dubbed one summer "The Summer of Kidnappings," even though, according to the National Center for Missing and Exploited Children, fewer kidnappings occurred that summer than in previous years. Subsequent media hype stories included the bird flu, which was supposed to wipe out the human race since the previous media hype, a disease known as "SARS," didn't.

Then, in 2007, we learned of the Mysterious Disappearance Of The Bees, which reached its peak when, according to a story I read on CNN's website, a Haagen-Dazs executive warned that a bee shortage could reduce the supply of ice-cream. (Really. The story is still on the site if you don't believe me.) Bees, the executive explained, are responsible for about 40% of the company's ice-cream flavors. That sounds disgusting at first, but the story goes on to clarify that what he meant was that roughly 40% of the flavors come from fruits and nuts, and without pollination by bees, the supply of those ingredients would drop, and then we would be faced with fewer choices of ice-cream flavors. Considering the pressing issues of our time—war, a shaky economy, high gas prices, declining *American Idol* ratings—an ice-cream shortage is something we simply do not have the resources to deal with right now.

We don't hear about the bees anymore, probably because the people who conduct the Bee Census found them after thousands of them (the bees, not the census takers) fled from the bush near my front door, where they were hiding out for a while, making it difficult for me to get into my own home. But you didn't tune in today to read about my personal problems so let's get back to the point.

As summer approaches, the news outlets are faced with a dilemma. Already this year the cable news channels have been broadcasting aerial shots of crowded beaches, telling viewers that the little black lines under the water are in fact sharks. Imagine that. Sharks! In the ocean!

But the problem for the media is this: Which story translates to higher ratings, the shark attacks or the rice shortage?

The what? Yes, apparently there's a rice shortage and if you go to some of the larger "box stores" like Costco and Sam's Club, you can purchase only four bags of rice per trip. That's it. You're limited to a meager four bags! Sure, these are twenty-pound bags we're talking about but is eighty pounds of rice, per customer, per trip, really enough for the average American?

Yes. But forget about that for now. We Americans don't want to be told that we shouldn't drive huge gas-guzzling cars; we don't want to be told what we should or shouldn't be able to watch on TV; and we sure don't want to be told how much rice we can have in our possession at any given time.

So if eighty pounds of rice per trip is not enough for you and your family, there's an easy way to get around this rationing. Order Chinese take-out, with extra rice. *Lots* of extra rice, as much as fifty or sixty of those little paper cartons, or however many they can fit in the delivery-person's car. The bonus in this plan is that this rice, unlike the rice you can't get at Costco anyway, is already cooked! So, yes, it will obviously cost more. Tell them you're willing to pay extra because your dinner consisting of one order of chicken and broccoli and one order of beef and broccoli will not be complete with two skimpy containers of rice. Being in business to make money, they will most likely oblige and sell you the rice.

If they give you any trouble ("Hey, you're trying to circumvent the rice rationing, aren't you!") stand up for your American self.

First, tell them that you're impressed that they used the word "circumvent." Then tell them that this is the USA, home of the "All You Can Eat Buffet." This isn't some third world country where the government sets the rules about how much food a person is allowed to consume. To prove this, tell them to look out the window. More than likely there will be an American out there on the sidewalk eating, perhaps even lying down, exhausted, next to the remnants of a pizza.

The person taking your order will then understand that this is not a place where the government tramples on the rights of its citizens. This is a country where we can have any amount of anything we want, including ice-cream produced by bees, if that's what we want. Which we don't. Trust us.

HOUSE HUNTERS

It is time to move again, which means unless I want to live in a tent or a refrigerator box, I have to find a permanent solid structure to keep my things in and also for sleeping.

Looking for such places seems to be the "in" thing to do, as evidenced by the television show *House Hunters*. If you've never seen it, you should check it out. It's on a cable network called "HGTV" which stands for "Humid Global Tenderloin Vortex." I frankly have no idea why anyone would start a cable network with that name but it seems to be working out for them.

At any rate, the show consists of people, usually a couple, being dragged around town by a real estate agent, followed by a camera crew (essential for TV) so they can view potential places to put their stuff in and sleep. The real estate agents on the show are usually very patient, putting up with their clients' various objections to different places, such as: "We like the classy spiral staircase, but it's missing several steps and this is only a one-story house." Rather than sighing very loudly and rolling their eyes, the real estate agents typically respect the clients' view and they go on to the next house, and another.

From what I gather, if you sign up to be on the show as a potential buyer, you're allowed to view only three houses. Some people might find this limiting, but they should also look at the upside: The entire process of house hunting—viewing houses, making offers and counter-offers, requesting repairs and/or upgrades, closing on the house, moving in—takes only *thirty minutes*. That's quite a deal.

At the end of those thirty minutes, the producers try to build in a little suspense before the last commercial break by teasing the audience with something like this: "Will Cathy and Darryl choose the brick home with the railroad tracks in the backyard? Will they go for the adorable modern house that has no garage or bathrooms? Or will they choose the quaint Tudor house with the indoor snake problem?"

I'm hoping to avoid all three kinds. It's not that I'm picky; I really only have a few things I look for in a home: quiet neighborhood, a somewhat updated interior and, of course, not haunted. Other than that, I'm pretty open-minded.

My co-hunter and I have been looking at places over the last couple of months and haven't found much that appeals to us. But last weekend we were driving around looking at places from the street (and getting odd looks from our potential future neighbors as we drove slowly down their tranquil, safe streets as though we were casing the place for prospective robbery targets) and found a place we both liked to look at from the street.

Unfortunately, we wouldn't be living outside the place and always looking at it from that viewpoint; we hope to be inside the house. So, without having a way in (again, the breaking-and-entering idea surfaces but I swear, we did not consider it) we were stuck with having to make contact with the real estate agent who listed the house.

I emailed the guy on Monday. Things did not turn out as I had hoped.

Mr. Snardle,
I'm writing concerning the listing at XXXXXXXX. There was no price in your listing, so before I bother you with too many questions, I'd like to know what they're asking.
Thanks,
Jeff

Dear Jeff, thanks for your interest. Unfortunately, we have accepted an offer from another buyer. Good luck in your search and if you need anything, please don't hesitate to ask.
Yours,
Jim

Jim,

May I call you Jim? At first I addressed you as "Mr. Snardle," but when you wrote back you just used "Jim" and also you called me "Jeff" rather than "Mr. Tompkins" so I assume we're on a first name basis. Anyway, thanks for getting back to me. Just out of curiosity, how much was the house going for?

Thanks,
Jeff

Mr. Tompkins, I didn't mean any disrespect. Sorry about that. The house was listed for $439,800. There are other houses in that same neighborhood for similar prices. Let me know if you would like to see them if you don't already have a realtor.

Yours,
Jim

Jimbo,
That price sounds great. We'll take it!
Jeff

Jeff, I don't know you and I certainly don't go by Jimbo. I assume you were joking about my name.......that is kind of odd to email someone so unprofessionally. Hopefully you were joking about taking the house too b/c it is not for sale. You asked what the price was and I told you what it sold for. Sorry for the confusion.

Yours,

Jim

Mr. Jimbo,

I apologize for the informality of "Jimbo." That was rude. You are correct; you don't know me and I guess I was too quick to move our friendship to the next level, although you do keep signing off with "Yours" which may have started us down this road. I accept your apology for creating the confusion about the price of the house and appreciate your taking responsibility for all of this. I now understand that it sold for $439,800. I would like to counter-offer and I'll start at $245,600. I realize that's kind of low but I'm a little short on cash. I recently purchased a boat and it sank. I didn't have insurance on it so the whole thing is a total loss. Also the marina keeps calling me and telling me I'm going to have to pay the bill for having someone haul it up from the ocean floor but they can keep begging, because honestly, what am I going to do with a sunken boat, you know? If I get another boat they will probably not let me keep it there but that's OK because they had a terrible snack bar anyway.

Jeff

Jeff, I meant that I don't go by Jimbo OR Mr. Jimbo. Putting Mr. in front of it doesn't make it better. I don't think you understand how realestate works. You can't make a counter offer on a house that is already sold for almost twice what you are offering. That just isn't how it works. I'm sorry to hear about your boat. Which marina was it? I keep mine at the Ashley Marina. Again if you need any listings or anything I will be happy to provide it for you.

Yours,
Jim

Mrs. Jimbo,

You are correct about my lack of understanding of real estate. The only thing I know about it is that it is two words, not one. Thank you for your kind words regarding what used to be my boat. The marina was up in North Carolina. I doubt you've ever heard of it. The marina, I mean. I'm sure you have heard of the state of North Carolina. It's just north of the state we are both currently in, hence the name. I'm kind of what you might call a boat connoisseur so I'd be very interested in hearing about your boat. What kind is it?

Jeff

Listen, Jeff. It's not Mrs. Jimbo either. Just call me JIM. I know you are probably just kidding around but I am busy and don't really have time for this. Of course I know what North Carolina is. My boat is a 84 foot Ocean Alexander motoryacht. Now if you have any serious need for a realtor let me know. Otherwise please stop with the messages about non related subjects.

Yours, Jim

JIM (better?),

I appreciate the information on your boat but there is no need to brag. Jeez.

Definitely Not Yours,
Jeff

~~~

SIDE EFFECTS

Lately I have become annoyed by medicine commercials. What? You say I have too much time on my hands? You may be right about that but if you're too busy to notice what those disclaimers are saying, then you're in for a big surprise someday.

For instance, a certain type of cold and flu medicine could produce the following side effects: runny nose, fever, aches and pains, cough, headache, sore throat, diarrhea and vomiting. So if you think you have a severe cold or flu (which you would recognize because you were experiencing runny nose, fever, aches and pains, cough, headache, sore throat, diarrhea and vomiting) then you should take the medicine that will make you feel better (after possibly causing you to experience side effects such as runny nose, fever, aches and pains, cough, headache, sore throat, diarrhea and vomiting).

To sum up this pharmaceutical company's message: "If you think you have a cold or flu, take our medicine and you will *know* you have it because we will ensure that you feel like crap, at which time we advise you to keep taking the medication to get rid of the symptoms that may or may not have been caused by us in the first place. Thank you."

It seems as though every medication can produce startling side-effects, everything from blurry vision to four-hour erections. Hopefully, those two never happen at the same time. Look out, ladies! (And men, if you're in a certain airport bathroom and a certain Republican senator shows up.)

The reason that these commercials list the possible side effects is to shield the company against potential lawsuits on the legal grounds that "we *told* you this headache remedy could cause you to sprout wings! But you took it anyway, even for a little headache, you wuss."

Another advertisement warns potential users of the drug that taking it regularly "may cause muscle spasms, eye twitching, itchy scalp and declining to accept an offer consisting of more money than you'd ever make in your natural life in exchange for opening just one more case that might hold a penny or a dollar on the hit show *Deal or No Deal*."

Perhaps the most famous medicine commercial was the one in which a guy appears on your screen (not mine, because I change the channel) and pitches some over-the-counter medication after telling you that he's not a doctor, he just plays one on TV. Due to a psychiatric phenomenon in which people do whatever someone on TV tells them to do (technical term: The Oprah Effect) millions of people rushed out to buy the product, only to be disappointed when they read the warning label and found out that the commercial failed to include this disclaimer: "The guy plays the title role on the show *Marcus Welby, M.D.*, and on more than one occasion told a patient not to worry about the bill. Ha ha! Doctors don't do that, you morons."

A commercial for a sleeping pill features a glow-in-the-dark butterfly that lands on the sleeping person's pillow. The drug, designed to help you fall asleep and stay that way, has a few side effects. The commercial ends with an advisory to stop taking the medicine if you experience headache, dry mouth, anxiety and a few other relatively mild symptoms. But it fails to mention whether you should stop taking the drug if you're seeing fluorescent butterflies in your bedroom. Sleep experts say that it is perfectly normal to hallucinate if you're taking this type of medication and the best way to avoid it is to "whack the butterfly with your hand or a blunt object, after making sure that you're not hitting the pillow of your spouse or whoever may be sleeping next to you, unless it is a certain Republican senator who followed you home from an airport bathroom."

Frankly, I'm kind of sick of these warnings on commercials. I'd like to see one in which the pharmaceutical company casts aside all concern about covering its butt, does not attempt to list the most alarming possible effects, and gets right to the point: "Do you have problems with excessive nasal discharge? If so, you are disgusting."

~~~

TAKE THIS SONG AND SHOVE IT

I have something to say to Minnie Riperton. What, you don't know who she is? Sure you do. She's the lady responsible for the song "Lovin' You." If you don't immediately recognize that song, it's the one that contains the following lyrics: "Lovin' you is easy cause you're beautiful."

I have heard this song on the radio maybe twice in my life, but probably somewhere around 30,000 times in my head because once you hear it, you can never forget it. And I mean that in the worst way.

"Lovin' you is easy cause you're beautiful"? Let's look at this line from both genders' perspectives.

Women don't want to hear that. Sure, they want to hear they're beautiful, even if they're not. Women don't want to be lied to, but this is one case in which some of them will make an exception. And I don't mean to single out the women who are not beautiful, but I don't really need to, do I?

If a man told a woman that she was easy to love because she's beautiful, he'd very likely face an inquiry not unlike being on the witness stand as a defendant in a mass murder trial. There's no getting out of that. Women, in my experience, want to be told that they are loved because they are caring, intelligent, interesting, humorous and all the other positive attributes that normally come to mind when a man is trying to convince a woman he loves her for more than her good looks.

From the male perspective (ladies, pay attention here because I'm about to divulge some classified material) it *is* easier to love a woman who is beautiful. If you're a woman and you object to that, please explain the phrase: "Love at first sight," which apparently does exist in one form or another, usually in movies seen on cable channels geared toward the female gender.

So women also find it easier to love a man who is beautiful, but, honestly, we don't want you to use that word. You might want to say something like this instead: "Lovin' you is easy cause you're good at sitting on the couch watching the playoffs." Trust me. We would love you if you said that! (Especially if you're beautiful when you say it.)

But that's not what I wanted to say to Minnie Riperton, if she's reading this, which I am pretty sure she isn't because she died in 1979. But if she were alive and I had just one question to ask her it would be: "Why did you think it was a good idea to include those tweeting birds in the song?" And if I had the chance to ask her two questions, the second would be: "When you sang the line 'No one else can make me feel the colors that you bring' what kind of powerful narcotics were you on? Because, really, what does it *mean*?"

While I'm on a music rant here, I might as well say something to Neil Sedaka, who is still alive. If you don't know who this guy is, he's the individual responsible for some of the catchiest songs ever written, two of which are "Calendar Girl" and "Breaking Up Is Hard To Do."

What I'd like to say to Neil is: "You make me want to gouge my eardrums out with an oyster fork."

If you've read this far and managed not to get these songs stuck in your head, congratulations. If you do have one or more running on a loop in your mind, please do not sing out loud. Also, don't blame me. Blame Minnie and Neil. And Barry Manilow, too, because he wrote that terrible Band-Aids jingle that you will have in your head all day now that I brought it up. You know: "I am stuck on Band-Aids...."

~~~

THE CASE AGAINST SUMMER

Spring is in the air. You can actually see it, in the form of a green powdery film that gets on everything from cars to pets—basically everything outside. And also everything *inside*, if you have the nerve to open your windows with the hope of getting some "fresh" air inside your house.

And with the arrival of spring, summer is just around the corner. I realize that I'm going to place myself in the minority here, but I'm going to explain why these two seasons comprise the worst part of the year.

I've already mentioned the pollen, even though it was probably unnecessary because you're almost certainly reading these words through teary eyes. You also might notice that it takes you twice as long to read this article. It's not that this is any longer than pieces I usually write, it's just that you will probably have to stop several times to sneeze and wipe your nose.

Pollen isn't the only sign, though. You may have noticed that people are starting to ask you, "Ready for the summer?" I don't know what kind of answer people are looking for when they ask this. Maybe something like, "Yes, I am! I gassed up the wave-runner just this morning and I'm wearing not only sunscreen but also a thin coat of shark-repellant!" I haven't tried that (the answer, not the shark-repellant) yet, but I might. For now, a simple "Yep, you?" seems to work. And then we go back to being the non-talking strangers we were meant to be.

This is also the time of year when you will see the first wave of the bugs of summer. I've already seen a few mosquitoes loitering around the light near my front door. Those are the big ones, the ones that have legs long enough to qualify them as the Kareem Abdul Jabbar of their species. The ones you can't see, the so-called "no-see-ems," are out in force as well, making holes in your family and friends before they can be detected.

Also, at least in the area where I live, we have the dreaded "palmetto bugs." Let's just call them what they are: roaches. The tourists will still come. Trust me. So far I have seen two roaches this season. One outside, one inside. You're going to think I'm making up the next part of this article, but I'm not, I swear.

One night, while writing, I heard what sounded like a rustling sound coming from the kitchen which is right next to my writing desk. The more I listened, the more I realized that the rustling was more like a crunching, but I couldn't figure out what it was. It was getting on my nerves to the point of distraction, so I walked into the kitchen and found a roach eating a cracker. I had apparently dropped a cracker at some point and it had fallen in the narrow space between the refrigerator and the counter. I stood there for a minute, waiting for more crunching, and within seconds I heard it again. If you think you're as sickened as I was, think again. I actually *heard the roach eating*.

This particular roach was so arrogant that it didn't even run away when I stomped near it. (Common advice you'll get from entomologists: "Stomp near it!") That was my only immediate recourse, as the space between the fridge and the counter was so small. And since I didn't have any bug spray in the house, I had to resort to drowning it in about 50 pumps from a bottle of Clorox Disinfecting Kitchen Cleaner. Only then, after a bit of dramatic flailing, did the roach succumb. Then I had to clean up not only a dead roach, but a dead roach that had just drowned in big puddle of kitchen cleaning chemicals. I guess I had it better than the roach; that couldn't have been a good way to go.

I haven't seen any roaches since. Maybe the word got out. *That guy is crazy! He won't stomp on you; he'll drown you in bleach!* Or maybe it's just luck on my part. Any day now I'm going to get home from the store and there will be a couple of brazen roaches—the really big ones that show up on airport radar systems—waiting at the door, tapping their watches, insisting that I drop another cracker. Maybe they'll be nice enough to help me bring the groceries in.

Everyone agrees that this is a bad time of year for bugs, but have you noticed the *people*? This is the season when everyone is sweating. Some of them even use the bottom of their shirt to swab their foreheads. I try not to do much outside during the summer (are you surprised?) but I do have to go outside, so I'm not saying that I don't sweat. What I'm saying is that I don't sweat and then go into a store, dripping wet, and leaving steamy forearm prints on counters that other people will be touching. Call me crazy, but I think society needs some "sweat etiquette" lessons. This should be a major government initiative.

I realize that I will find some disagreement from you "summer people" who like boating, fishing, swimming, sunburn, heat strokes, severe B.O., 300% humidity, thunderstorms, lightning, tornadoes, hurricanes, giant roaches, ferocious swarms of mosquitoes (and tourists) and an incalculable increase in traffic. I think the heat has done something to your brains.

I proudly admit to being the Scrooge of Summer.

~~~

WARNING! IGNORE AT YOUR OWN PERIL

It's time to start tracking the national IQ. This pressing need has nothing to do with the fact that many Americans are incapable of parking within the lines or because Regis is still on the air. It has to do with product warning labels.

A few nights ago I was in the kitchen doing some routine bachelor cleaning (making circular wiping motions on the counter with a wet paper towel, sweeping crumbs under the refrigerator, chiseling congealed glops of something off the floor) and I noticed the warning on a bottle of a popular cleaning fluid: "DO NOT SPRAY INTO EYES."

The timing couldn't have been better. Having nearly completed the cleaning, I was thinking: While I'm at it, I might as well bleach my eyes.

Of course I am kidding. But apparently someone has done this, or at least the company had good reason to believe that someone might. Warning labels are put on products as legal disclaimers in the hopes that when some mouth-breather uses lighter fluid as a marinade and gets sick, the company can deflect a potential lawsuit by saying, "Didn't you read the warning label? It clearly says: 'DO NOT SOAK FOOD IN THIS.'"

Other items around my house that have interesting warning labels include:

Febreeze: "DO NOT SPRAY DIRECTLY TOWARD FACE" (indirectly, sure, but not directly)

Germ-X antibacterial wipes: "In case of accidental ingestion…" (are people "accidentally" eating these things?)

Glade room air-freshener: "DO NOT EAT" (but it smells so good!)

Iron: "Do not iron clothes on body" (even though it's so much more convenient, and you can also see how it will really look on you)

Old Spice deodorant: "Not for intimate hygiene use" (not that there's anything wrong with that)

Fire extinguisher: "Operating too close to fire may result in personal injury" (in other words: "Do not get too close to fire, as if you shouldn't already know that!")

I was a bit concerned when I discovered a few items that were missing some much-needed warnings, considering how dumb the general public must be.

For instance, the package of light bulbs should carry this warning: "Do not put in paper bag and smash with hammer creating tiny shards of glass and swallowing them or pouring directly into eyes."

I have several packs of blue medium-point Bic ballpoint pens that should carry this warning: "Do not jab into face or major critical organs."

Also, there's nothing on my TV warning me not to lift it off the table and drop it on my head. My car does not contain a warning about putting it in gear, getting out, and jumping under the wheels. The razors in my bathroom drawer do not have a warning about the potential hazards of using them as an ingredient in banana bread. My phone did not come with a warning about the futility of trying to reach a customer service rep who has half a clue as to how to assist me.

You get the point…unless you're one of those people who might try using a turkey fryer in your bedroom or if you're one of those kids who inspired the costume company to include a warning with a Superman costume: "Cape does not enable you to fly," or if you need a warning on your dashboard sunshield telling you to remove it before operating your vehicle.

The point of course is that we are surrounded by morons: people who think the warning on Q-tips packaging about pushing them too far into your ear is a mere suggestion, people who give their pet a bath and consider drying them in the oven, and people who use insect spray in unventilated confined areas such as the plastic bags they have over their heads.

I say it's time to start figuring the national IQ, not only so we can be aware of exactly how dangerous it is to be around the average imbecile, but also because it's a matter of national security. If we made this statistic public, our enemies may very well leave us alone. They might decide that their efforts are just not worth it. "Ha ha," they will say, "why spend all our time and money attacking them when they are terrorizing themselves with ordinary household items? We can stay right here in our village and relax! Now get me a piece of that banana bread someone sent to us."

~~~

WEB OF CONCEIT

It's October, and Halloween is coming, so it is in that spirit that I figured it's time to talk about The Spider Wars.

Let me state here, right at the beginning, for anyone who may be inclined to denounce my actions described later in this column, that I respect spiders. I have nothing against them, per se. I realize they perform valuable functions in our ecosystem, such as suddenly appearing on your shoulder while you're watching TV, and making sticky webs that get stuck on your face if you walk through them.

And after doing some research I gained even more respect for these creatures. For instance, I learned that spiders have a pair of appendages near the mouth called "pedipalps," and, according to one article I read, they can sometimes "look like boxing gloves, depending on sex." Frankly, I do not care how much sex a spider is getting, but it was interesting all the same.

Speaking of that, I learned that the mating habits of spiders are usually very elaborate. Some of it seemed a bit outlandish to me, and probably more trouble than it's worth. Example: one of the most fascinating things about the mating ritual is that many female spiders will kill their male partners after the act. Scientific research shows that the females do this because, after the mating process (technical term: spider lovin') the males want to go home and sleep in their own beds rather than cuddle with the female. This leads to an argument, and the female asks, "Will you at least call me?" The male looks at his watch (researchers don't know why he does this) and says, "Sure." Then the female spider says, "'Sure'? That's it? You're telling me 'sure'?" And then she tears his head off.

Recent studies show that the males have it coming. As one leading spider expert put it, "They deserve it…big time."

But back to the point of this column. (At least, I think there's a point. If you find one, let me know.)

About a month ago, a spider decided that the best place to spin a web would be just outside my door. I had not been notified that this was going to take place, so one morning I found out via the aforementioned method of walking through part of the web and then flailing my arms trying to get the web off my face.

Once I had done that and could see straight again, I found a stick and destroyed the web. Though I had not seen an actual spider, I was relieved and went on with my life.

A couple of weeks later, again in the early morning hours, I noticed that the web was back, built in the same place. I got another stick (or maybe the same one; I don't keep a stick inventory) and once again set about destroying the web.

This new and improved web was very strong and I assumed that the spider had constructed it that way because we were about to enter the peak of hurricane season. If you're a spider with a weak web, and it's the time of year when tropical winds can destroy your living quarters, it can be very difficult to get insurance. So I knew I was dealing with a smart one.

This time I saw the actual spider, though I had no idea what kind it was. I'm familiar with a few types of spiders, such as the Black Widow, Daddy Long Legs, and even his lesser known relative, Mama Medium Legs. But I couldn't identify this spider by name. It was orange and brown, and roughly the size of a mouse, only with more hair.

So much hair, in fact, that it appeared to be wearing a stole made of giraffe fur. And the more I think about it, that might actually be the case. Based on the fact that this spider rebuilt a web in the same place where his or her old one was foreclosed upon, I knew this was a very egotistical spider, and if it wanted a giraffe, it would get one.

The spider moved down the web, closer to me, as if challenging me to a fight. I reacted to this with a slight chuckle for a couple of reasons.

First, was I really supposed to be scared? Well, I wasn't, even if it did have pedipalps that looked like boxing gloves. While I wasn't frightened, though, I was a little worried. I've been to an emergency room before but not for treatment after being boxed in the face by a spider, and that would be slightly difficult and embarrassing to explain.

Second, there was simply no way I was going to get into the web, no matter how much it taunted me. What a ridiculous expectation on the part of that spider. I still can't believe it was thinking that. What a fool!

I knew I couldn't let the spider stay where it was, so I had to come up with a plan.

The first option, in keeping with my feelings about nature and life and my respect for the balance of the ecosystem, was to use the stick to carefully pound the spider into a rather disgusting heap of spider innards and giraffe hair.

But I ruled that out. What had the spider done to deserve such a cruel death? Nothing, as far as I know. So I decided instead to coax the spider into climbing aboard the stick, whereupon I would relocate it into the woods (behind someone else's home, of course) and let it go.

That's pretty much what I did, and I'll leave it at that. Not only because that's the happy ending, but also because it saves me from mentioning here publicly that I made some exceedingly non-masculine verbal noises during the process.

~~~

WHO ARE YOU WEARING?

Unlike hockey season, which begins on September 29th and ends on September 28th of the following year, the entertainment industry packs its awards season into a span of five or six weeks. It includes the Golden Globes, which was invented by Hugh Hefner and was originally a show that gave out awards for only one category: Best Cleavage; the SAG Awards, which is not an acronym but an accurate description of the original intent of the event, which was to give awards to actors over the age of 80 (this is also why SAG is in all capital letters…much easier to read); and the Grammy Awards, viewed by several dozen adults worldwide, along with every teenager with the energy to have that time-honored hallucination of youth that they too can form a band even though their preparation for a career in music consists solely of growing long hair and smoking pot.

The Awards Show Season ends with the Oscars, the occasion famous for honoring life-long dreams, but only for thirty-eight seconds, at which time the recipients will be cut off by orchestra music. If these Hollywood stars are so creative, why haven't any of them come up with the idea that when the music starts, they should begin singing their speeches? If they were serious about thanking everyone, they would try it. And if they were really serious about it, they would hire one of those fast-talking voiceover guys who read the disclaimers at the end of car commercials.

The same part of my brain that causes me to wonder what would happen if I put an unopened orange juice container in the microwave caused me to tune in to the Academy Awards red carpet show. And who did I see but Hollywood's ubiquitous professional host and red carpet stalker, Ryan Seacrest.

Ryan, who is 3'11" (in his high heels), stood on a stack of Los Angeles metro telephone books, interviewing the stars as they arrived for the festivities. This was a good move, because last year he was embarrassed when stars put their bottled water and handbags on his head when they stopped to talk to other interviewers.

That's what I was told, anyway, because I had never watched one of these shows until tonight. I can't remember much of what was said because I was distracted by a question I kept hearing: "*Who* are you wearing?"—a question that sounds like it was asked by someone who doesn't know how to properly use interrogative and relative pronouns. You would think that would be one of the requirements for hosting something as important as the Oscars red carpet show. I mean, come on. This isn't the Grammys.

Now, of course I knew what he meant. He was asking them who designed their clothing. I don't remember any of the answers, because most of them were foreign names and I'm sure some of them were made up on the spot.

Ryan: Who are you wearing?
Actor: This is Petit Bébé L'orange.

And Ryan would respond with a thoughtful nod, unaware that the actor had just told him that his suit was designed by a little orange baby.

The posing of this question would be the perfect opportunity for someone to walk up to Ryan while giving Jack Nicholson a piggy-back ride and answer: "Jack Nicholson. I'm wearing Jack Nicholson!" But I knew that would never happen so I had to come up with another reason to keep watching. And that's when I realized that I should keep watching for the same reason people watch auto racing. No, not because I drank a case of beer and was suddenly fascinated with traffic. People watch racing for the crashes. And so I found my excuse: Watch the Oscars with the hope that someone important falls down.

It's not too much to ask. All it would take is one of the actresses walking out on stage and getting her dress tangled between her shoes, and down she goes.

Then Seacrest could run out on stage, put the microphone in her face and ask, "*Who* did you just trip over?"

~~~

COOL TO BE KIND

If you're like me (and God help you if you are) you had no idea that Friday was World Kindness Day. I became aware of this in the middle of the day, so if anyone in charge of World Kindness Day happens to read this, please excuse me for not being kind until around 2:30 p.m. EST.

According to the official World Kindness Day website, this day is observed every year on November 13. The page notes: "This was the opening day of the first

World Kindness Movement® conference held at Tokyo in 1998, and the 35th anniversary of the Small Kindness Movement of Japan, which brought the signatories of the 'declaration of kindness' of the World Kindness Movement together in 1997."

You may remember from your history books (or Wikipedia, I can't remember which) that the Declaration of Kindness was the name of the first draft of the Declaration of Independence, but during the editing process one of the alert (read: not drunk) members of the Second Continental Congress realized that something was wrong.

"This isn't supposed to be nice," he said. "We're declaring independence here! And who wrote the opening sentence, *We hold these truths to be self-evident, if you don't mind*? That's too nice. No kindness!" And thus a nation was born.

But back to this current Declaration of Kindness... I think the world could use more stuff like this. And while I'm at it, I would like to say that the world needs better TV shows and also more types of cheese dips. But I suppose those things can wait while we solve other, more important problems in the world such as eradicating terrorism and country music.

Anyway, the website states that the purpose of World Kindness Day is not simply to be kind to people, but to consider people outside of our own race, religion and culture, and realize that focusing on our common humanity will bring about a more peaceful world. People interested in this peace movement are also encouraged to spread kindness to others, by force if necessary.

No, I kid the peace movement! I made up that last part. I know some people might read that and take offense, but as is often the case when I make a light-hearted joke about using force to spread peace, I would just ask you to be kind to me, in the name of peace, and forget that I wrote it. Okay?

The truth is, I believe in kindness. If you underestimate the importance of kindness, consider this: You're in a restaurant and the waiter brings your meal consisting of a steak and a baked potato. This is what you ordered. But on top of the potato, there is a sprig of something green that you cannot immediately identify. You're sure that you did not order the green sprig or any color sprig for that matter. But there it is. Right on top of your potato.

The server comes by three or four minutes later and asks, "You still working on that? Can I get you a to-go box? Will this be on the same check or separate?" Here you have a choice: you can elect to ignore the problem on the potato, or you can make an issue of it. This is where kindness comes into play.

If you're a kind person, you remain calm and politely inform them that you're still eating and everything's fine and you're not yet ready for the check. You say nothing about the fact that this sever is trying to hurry you so they can turn the table. Then, when the server leaves, you move the sprig to the side of your plate or, better yet, drop it under the table in a covert manner, while giving your date a conspiratorial look, hoping she'll get a laugh out of it and you'll score some points for being humorous in a playfully devious way.

If, however, you're not a kind person you make a scene, saying something like, "You just dropped off the food, idiot. Of *course* I'm still *working* on it." You then ask, "What kind of chef is back there sending out green sprigs that nobody ordered?" To which the confused young server says, "Sprig?" And then you go on to further insult the chef for putting a leafy branch of something on your potato, while also berating the server for their dismal vocabulary. You are now wasting the server's time, delaying important drink refills at other tables, word is getting back to the chef that he or she should come out and get a look at you so the next time you come in they can spit in your food, and while all of this is going on your date quietly slips away from the table and is outside calling a friend to come pick her up.

That is the type of horrible thing that can happen when people are not kind to each other. It's not quite the Israeli/Palestinian situation, but since most of us don't live over there, the restaurant situation is much easier to grasp. I'm confident that we've all known people who would do that kind of thing.

The point of all of this was just to let you know that last Friday was World Kindness Day, and you probably missed it. Judging by the behavior of the general public, pretty much everyone missed it. Or, more likely in this society, they ignored it. I have no illusions about this culture shedding its malicious tendencies, so with that in mind I offer this reminder: You have only 363 days until the next day of mandated kindness. So go forth and get in people's faces!

~ ~ ~

DIG THIS

They are digging outside my house. By "they" I mean demons from hell. No, that's not right. Demons from hell would never create such a racket.

I received a notice on my door about two weeks ago informing me that there would be crews in the area performing "a routine upgrade of the electrical distribution system." They didn't say when it would begin, so it was anyone's guess, including probably the people who were supposed to do the work. They also did not mention when the project would be completed, which is understandable, as they probably couldn't put too fine a point on it. As with any project of this sort, it will probably be wrapped up sometime between noon and four months from now.

I have two problems with this: 1) The electricity is working fine. As far as we, the consumers, can tell, there is no need to upgrade anything. 2) There is no need to inform me that crews would be working the area because I would become aware of this when they started up the machines, which turned out to be quite early in the morning, approximately one millisecond after the construction noise ordinance expired.

I was curious about the noise ordinance in my area, so I checked the city's website and the most recent reference I could find was a copy of the minutes of a committee meeting held several years ago in which the participants were discussing a change in the noise law. The existing law prohibited construction work between 11 p.m. and 6 a.m. Yes, you read that correctly. A construction crew could, at the time, begin work at 6 a.m.

I called City Hall to find out what the current noise regulation is.

Me: I'd like to speak to someone who can explain the city's noise ordinance as it relates to construction projects.

City Person: *Noise ordinance?* Ha! We don't have one. Construction crews can do anything they want, including blocking off roads with orange cones, even if there is no visible construction going on in the area.

No, seriously, when I called I was transferred only three times before a City Person was able to tell me, authoritatively, that they had no idea what the noise ordinance was. So I was transferred again and got a friendly City Person who told me that the current ordinance states that construction crews can begin working at 7 a.m.

So I guess I have nothing to complain about, and no one to complain *to*, as it relates to the law. But since construction crews are allowed to begin work at 7 a.m., they're defining "begin work" very loosely. Before the actual work begins, they have to get everything in place. That means the noise really starts about 6:30 or so, which is what happened this morning, when the crew started setting up.

I'm not exaggerating when I tell you that they were only about ten yards from my bedroom window. Oh, did I forget to mention that the memo I received a couple of weeks ago also said: "Crews will be working in yards (front, side, and/or back)"? They were just outside my bedroom window this morning, before 7 a.m., setting up something that I would later find out is called a "Ditch Witch." This is a machine that, despite its name, is not as pleasant as a witch. When the crew started it up, it sounded as though someone was out there testing the rocket boosters used on the Space Shuttle.

At precisely 7 a.m., the real work began. One member of the crew painted lines in the grass. Another member walked behind him, apparently providing needed backup in case something went horribly wrong during this critical phase of the operation. One guy got on the Ditch Witch in an apparent effort to see how loud it could be revved up. (Results: Very loud.) Five or six other guys performed the essential construction job of standing near the truck.

The truck, which was the approximate size of the aircraft-carrier Yorktown, apparently brought the Ditch Witch to the site. A good thing, too, because that was one less construction machine on the road during the morning rush hour. We've all been in traffic behind one of those construction machines making its way to a destination somewhere hundreds of miles away, ensuring that you'll be behind it the entire time. The machines always hold up traffic, creating what looks like a 300-car funeral procession led by a yellow, mud-encrusted bulldozer. Traffic moves so slowly that you're passed by an advancing column of ants.

I can't wait to see the improvement in the "electrical distribution system" when this project is completed. Maybe my lamps will turn on faster. I don't know.

What I do know, upon examining the notice that I received a few weeks ago (and which I kept, for some reason), is that there are several names and phone numbers listed on it. These are people I can contact if I have any questions or concerns.

Now that I know the names of the people who are responsible for this project, they aren't just "workers" to me—they're actual human beings who are just doing their jobs. I hope they are never stunned out of their sleep by the rumblings of a construction machine. And I hope they never find out that when I finish writing this I'm going to look up their addresses and then find out where I can rent a Ditch Witch.

Just kidding! Sort of....

~~~

HOW *NOT* TO WRITE A "HOW-TO" ARTICLE

It was every writer's dream: Someone wanted to pay me actual American dollars to write some articles for their publication. As you can imagine, I was pretty thankful to get this opportunity. That is, until I was told that the article would be about hands-free automatic balloon inflating instructions. (Whatever that is.) (And, no, I am not kidding about the topic.)

Here's what happened: I accepted a job offer as a freelance writer. Here's what else happened: I failed to fully research the media outlet I would be writing for. And by "fully research" I mean "didn't research at all."

This isn't the first time something like this has happened to me. One of my first jobs was through a "temp service," which is code for a company hiring you without having to give you benefits. The job was about thirty minutes from home and while the time spent in the car would be an annoyance, the travel cost wasn't a hindrance because this was back when you could afford a full tank of gas without having to sell a major bodily organ.

When I arrived at the job I was told that I would be organizing a warehouse, which didn't sound good, and in fact *wasn't* good, because it involved operating a forklift. The people at the temp service had, for some reason, failed to ask me if I knew how to operate a forklift, which I didn't. I don't think I had even been near a forklift, save for some instances of trivial vandalism when I was much younger. So long ago, in fact, that the statute of limitations has long expired, which is why I'm free to mention it here.

Anyway, I listened intently to the warehouse manager's instructions and thirty minutes later, when everything had been explained to me, when I was ready to get into the forklift and get to work, when the manager went to another part of the building to do something, I promptly located the nearest door, slipped out, and went home.

Now, I'm not an expert in job placement, but it seems to me that if you're hiring someone to drive a forklift, rather than having the applicant go through roughly two hours of personality tests and a computer proficiency exam, you could cut to the chase and ask, "Hey, can you drive a forklift?" But that never came up.

It would also make sense that if you're going to hire a freelance writer, you would ask the writer if he or she is interested in writing articles about any of the following topics, which I swear are actual writing assignments I was presented with:

—Assembly Instructions for Harness Type Hang Gliders

—How Can I Make an Electric Heating Pad?

—How to Build a Small Jet Engine Out of a Car Turbocharger

—Bowel Blockage Symptoms & Swallowing

—How to Measure Scrotum for a Suspensory

—Information on Solar Powered Hot Dog Cookers

—What Is the Buildup on Finches Behinds?

—How to Move Your Laundry Room Downstairs

—How to Measure the Thickness of a Head Gasket

—How to Build a Barn Area for a Milking Cow

Aren't those some fascinating topics? Wouldn't you jump at an opportunity like that? Perhaps even jump at it out of a window in a very tall building?

You probably noticed that several of those topics require mechanical and construction knowledge. And if you know me personally or if you read my writing on a regular basis, you're no doubt aware that when it comes to these two things I do not possess what you would call "knowledge" about either of those topics.

I'd be more likely to take two of the topics, such as "How to Measure Scrotum for a Suspensory" and "Information on Solar Powered Hot Dog Cookers," combine them, and write an article like "How to Measure a Scrotum Using a Hot Dog Cooker" or something like that. (Not that I would know about that either. I swear!)

I would also probably produce an article combining two other topics and it would be titled: "All Clear Below—Bowel Blockage Symptoms While Riding Around In a Hang Glider."

If I were to write an article for "How Can I Make an Electric Heating Pad?" it would go something like this: "You don't *make* a heating pad; you *buy* a heating pad. Go to Wal-Mart or Target, you cheap moron."

As for the "What Is the Buildup on Finches Behinds?" topic, I can't say for sure but I can make a guess. We're dealing with two things here: 1) a bird, and 2) some kind of build-up on its rear parts, so I'm going to go with the idea that it has something to do with (I know this is a stretch here) bird poop.

I couldn't write seriously about "How to Move Your Laundry Room Downstairs" because it's something that would never cross my mind. As far as I'm concerned, the laundry room stays where it is. I also couldn't write an informational article about measuring head gaskets because, to be technical about it, I have no idea what those are.

So obviously I was the wrong person for that writing job. But it's not entirely my fault. As I acknowledged, I didn't research this company very well, but they also didn't research me very well. If they had, they'd know that people don't read my articles to find out about milking a cow or hang-gliding; they read my articles to find out about milking a cow *while* hang-gliding.

~~~

NOTHING MORE THAN FEELINGS

A few weeks ago there was a big media brouhaha (Latin for "kerfuffle") over some leaked documents about the war in Afghanistan. The papers were released by an organization called Wikileaks, which sounds like it could be the name of one of those dolls that pees, but is not.

The incident raised several important questions, namely: Why are we still in Afghanistan? Is it really worth the cost, both financially and in terms of lives lost? Why do people buy dolls that pee, for God's sake?

No one really knows the answers to those questions, so I'm going to skip over them and get to the point I want to make today, which is that I have some very important classified information that I'm going to leak right here in this space, and we'll see just how serious our media is by how much coverage it gets.

I should start out by explaining that I decided to leak this information after coming to the conclusion that women think men have no feelings. This occurred to me after having conversations with a few women who displayed somewhat negative points of view about men, usually in the form of a statement like this: "Men suck."

One of these women expressed that belief after viewing a very important sociological documentary called "The Bachelorette." In the interest of full disclosure I need to point out that I also saw the show, and have no problem admitting it publicly, especially here in the fourth paragraph, because if anyone was bored by the first, second or third paragraphs of this article, they've stopped reading by now which means I'll face fewer people ridiculing me for having watched the program.

If you're not familiar with the show, all you need to know is that it consists of one female being courted by somewhere around dozen men, and throughout the season she goes on "dates" with them and then, just like real-world dating, she rips their hearts out and eats them. No, wait. Sorry. I let a little personal bias slip into the explanation. What really happens is that she sends one or more guys home every episode, until she's left with just one guy who then proposes to her.

What got this female friend of mine so irate was that during this season of the show, the bachelorette found out that a couple of the guys already had girlfriends. The nerve! I mean, here's this girl who puts her life on hold to find Mr. Right, simultaneously dating a dozen or so guys, having romantic dinners with them, holding hands with them, kissing them, and spending some nights with a few of them in something called a "Fantasy Suite."

Meanwhile, a couple of no-good, heartless guys were interested in other women. What does a woman have to do these days to keep men faithful while she's off with other guys?

That's the question I asked my female friend, to which she responded, "OH MY GOD! You don't get it!"

The conversation went back and forth over the issue of whether or not I get it, with me calmly offering highly-rational points, such as: "If she's doing all this romantic stuff, including physical contact, with other guys, why did she freak out when a couple of guys were into other girls? Don't you see the hypocrisy in that?" and getting responses such as: "Men—you all suck!"

Okay, fine, I might be slightly biased in my account of the conversation, but what it all boils down to is the fact that women think men have no feelings. Perhaps this is because men just don't express their feelings as often as women do. Perhaps it's because some women have had experiences with a guy or two who treated them badly and the women concluded that the only reason a man would do that is because he has no feelings and can't even comprehend the notion that other people do.

Or perhaps it's because of the research done at Harvard Medical School, wherein probes were inserted into the brains of women and men, and the results showed that the vast majority of women's emotions were related to nurturing, love and affection, while the vast majority of men's emotions were related to bad calls by referees, what's for dinner and (this probably goes without saying) breasts.

A-ha! See, I made up that Harvard study, but I know some of you women out there were nodding your heads as though you finally had confirmation for your suspicions about the thoughts of men. And why is that? Well, as luck would have it, the Johns Hopkins University School of Medicine just released a study that shows women believe those things about men because they *want* to believe those things about men. Okay, I made up that study, too. (But we all know it's true.)

Back to the point, which is the classified information I want to reveal.

WARNING! EYES ONLY – CLASSIFIED INFORMATION TO FOLLOW

Men have feelings, too.

That's right, ladies. We men experience feelings too. Sure, we may not feel them *exactly* like you do. For instance, very few men experience the emotion that causes us to say "Awwwww" every time we see a baby. Nor do most of us experience an emotion that comes anywhere close to causing us to believe there's the slightest justification for the existence of those things you call "doilies."

Those are two examples of how we're different, and of course there are more, but generally speaking those of us in the male gender can experience things like love, heartache, devotion, disappointment, desire, blah blah blah, etc.

Be as skeptical as you want, but I want to close by emphasizing that the result of that fictitious Harvard study is completely untrue.

Well…most of it, anyway.

~~~

OUTTA SIGHT

I knew I had a problem when I was watching a football game and heard commentary that included phrases such as: "He's gonna put the six ball in the corner pocket." I've been a football fan my entire life and despite having heard the commentators use pool metaphors like "This team has to run the table," I was pretty sure there are no pockets in the corners of the field.

Okay, I'm exaggerating. I wasn't really watching televised billiards by mistake, although if I had been, that would have been my excuse. I was using hyperbole to make the point that my glasses were no longer keeping up with my deteriorating eyesight. This was probably because I get an annual eye exam about once per decade.

I seem to put off getting new glasses until things reach a critical stage. For instance, the last time I got new ones, ten years ago, it was only because a cat had run off with my glasses and, I guess, hidden them somewhere so she could melt them down and make a shank or whatever pets do with our missing stuff when we're not around.

Having poor eyesight and no glasses qualified as one of those "critical stages." It was probably all for the best anyway; that pair of glasses had "1980s" written all over them. Not literally. At least as far as I could tell; I couldn't really see them.

I don't know why I procrastinate when it comes to getting an eye checkup. It's no worse than going to the doctor and certainly nowhere near as bad as going to the dentist. As far as I know, the vast majority of optometrists do not put on rubber gloves and put their hands on certain personal body parts, nor do they use drills. Regardless, I'm just not a fan of medical visits. But a while back I ended up going anyway and it wasn't as bad as I thought.

The doctor began by ordering me to look into a machine and press a button when I saw some bright dots and flashes. I don't like this test because I see bright dots and flashes on a regular basis anyway, due in part to frequent headaches, which I probably have because I don't get my eyes checked when I should. So there I was, pushing the button, wondering if the dots and flashes were really there, and also whether the doctor might be thinking I was on LSD. (Legal disclaimer: I was not.)

Then it was time for her to blow the puff of air into my eye (official medical code-name: "Optical Gust"). Eye doctors claim this test detects signs of glaucoma, but I have my doubts. I think there's a good chance they do it as some kind of prank. And I swear I'm not just saying that because it's exactly what I would do if I were an optometrist. Or maybe it's some kind of experiment they're doing in conjunction with human behavior researchers to see what percentage of people will let a stranger attack their eyeballs with violent bursts of air. Turns out the answer is: 100%.

Having survived that procedure we moved on to the "Reading Of The Chart On A Faraway Wall While Holding A Plastic Thing Over One Eye" phase of the exam. I could easily make out the letters on the first line, which were "EZRMQP" but I had no idea how to pronounce that word, so I just read each individual letter and the doctor was fine with that. "Very good," she said, in a tone people usually reserve for babies or pets.

This went on for the next couple of rows, but then I got to one that was a little less clear, by which I mean it resembled a single-file line of fleas marching across the chart, but I didn't say that out loud for fear of confirming that LSD thing.

The doctor mercifully ended the exam at that point and told me I could come back to pick up my new glasses in about a week, which meant I would have to continue going around like the cartoon character Mr. Magoo for a while.

I have the new glasses now, and they're great. I'm noticing all kinds of visual details I hadn't seen before, such as my couch.

~~~

SPELLING BEEEEZZZZ

I want to point out that I did have something more important to do, but as is often the case, I just didn't feel like doing it. That's how, a few nights ago, I caught a few of minutes of a televised spelling bee. A couple of questions came to mind: 1) Why do they call it a "spelling bee"? 2) How can we make it more exciting, something really worthy of airing on TV?

I had plenty of time to let my mind wander, because there was very little actual spelling going on in the spelling bee. Instead, the contestants spent an inordinate amount of time asking questions about the word they were being asked to spell, as you can see in this 87% accurate excerpt from the transcript:

Moderator: Spell the word "guerdon."

Contestant: (sigh) Can you tell me the language of origin?

Moderator: French.

Contestant: (sigh, starting to cry a little) Can you give me the part of speech?

Moderator: Noun.

Contestant: (deep breath) Can you use it in a sentence?

Moderator: Yes. Here is your sentence: Spell the word "guerdon" or you *lose*.

OK, so that wasn't *exactly* how it went when "guerdon" came up, but a few stern threats like that from the judges would have made it more entertaining to watch.

The Scripps National Spelling Bee official website offers this explanation of the term "spelling bee":

The word bee, as used in spelling bee, is a language puzzle that has never been satisfactorily accounted for. A fairly old and widely-used word, it refers to a community social gathering at which friends and neighbors join together in a single activity (sewing, quilting, barn raising, etc.), usually to help one person or family. The earliest known example in print is a spinning bee, in 1769. Other early occurrences are husking bee (1816), apple bee (1827), and logging bee (1836). Spelling bee is apparently an American term. It first appeared in print in 1875.

I grant you that it doesn't give us a definitive answer, but at least we learned some fascinating information, such as the fact that at some point in our history, people were so bored they actually held quilting contests and barn building competitions. I'm going to go out on a limb here and guess that these events were free to spectators. This just doesn't sound exciting to me. But I suppose in those days people had enough excitement, in terms of simply trying to stay alive in the face of threats such as various pox-related diseases and also the possibility of being dragged off into the woods by a bear. Ah, simpler times.

But getting back to my point about the term "spelling bee"…I have an idea, one that will not only make the term clearer but will also make the competition much more entertaining.

Let's have spelling bees with actual bees. No, I don't mean as contestants, although judging by some of the spelling we encounter on a daily basis, the bees might actually defeat some humans.

What I propose is having the contestants spell the words while covered with bees. After having a bee expert smear them with whatever pheromone it is that makes bees swarm around something, the contestants would enter a glass box containing thousands of bees. The contestants would remain in the Bee Box, asking all the time-wasting questions they want (Language of origin? Part of speech? Can these bees get *inside my head*?), and then attempt to spell the word.

If they get it right, they're released from the box and they move on to the next round. If they get it wrong, they're released from the box and are eliminated from the competition. Ha! No, of course I am kidding. What fun would that be? Under my plan, they have to stay in the Bee Box until they spell the word correctly. We should be very strict about this. Spelling is very important and the future of our nation could depend on it.

But more importantly, it would make great TV. Although, I'm sure there's at least one attorney out there who would find a minor flaw in the plan and rush to the site of the contest to stop the proceedings. We cannot let that happen, and that's exactly why we would have a second *secret* Bee Box…

~~~

TALE OF AN ADORING FAN

This all began when I made a lighthearted comment about Connie Francis. For those of you who don't know who she is, don't worry—nobody does.

Actually, that's not true. Plenty of people know who she is. And, for the most part, they are all over the age of 60. See, Connie Francis was the top female musical artist of the 1950s and 1960s. (I got that fact from her Wikipedia page.) There are other ~~coma-inducing~~ fascinating facts about her, some of which we'll get to in a minute.

But first, a little background. A couple of weeks ago I was reading a blog that linked to a story about Connie Francis promoting some kind of upcoming beach party somewhere in Florida. She was on a float or in a convertible, along with several young men who, for whatever reason, forgot to put on their shirts that day. Ms. Francis and these men were advertising the beach party that coincides with the 50th anniversary of the movie *Where the Boys Are,* which featured a song by the same name, which was sung by—you guessed it—Barry Manilow.

Just kidding. It was performed by Connie Francis.

It turns out that the male models who were hired were actually gay porn stars. It also turns out that the city was not aware of this fact; they had meant to hire regular models. Hey, it happens. Incidentally, the mayor, before this was known, told reporters that the event would be "good old-fashioned family fun."

Anyway, in the comments section under the story, where many jokes were being made about the incident, I wrote that perhaps she was promoting a new movie called *Where The Girls Aren't (Except for Connie Francis) (Whoever She Is)*.

A few days later I got the following email from a guy named Sal:

I read your comment about Connie on the Where The Boys Are article. I cannot believe that you do not know who she is. She is the third top selling female vocalist of all time with 56 chart hits in the US alone. She was the top female concert act throughout the 60s and continues to sell out. Up until the 90s, she was just behind the Beatles and Elvis in sales.

Sal had apparently followed the link back to my blog, where he located my email address and felt a strong urge to defend Ms. Francis. I always respond to emails so I wrote:

I apologize. I am not familiar with many of the washed-up entertainers from the mid-1900s, but now I know who Connie is. Her PR team is doing a great job managing her comeback, having her promote beach parties by riding around on a float with some of South Florida's finest porn actors. Maybe Elvis should try that.

I thought that wound be the end of it, but our correspondence continued for the better part of an hour. Here's what happened:

SAL: Her management is making a big mistake. She has never believed in PR until now. She is not as washed up as you think. She still makes millions in concerts and is working on a big deal in Vegas. She recently was the biggest draw in Vegas and Atlantic City. Wherever she goes, she is a sell out and she recently sang to 25,000 people in the Far East, and to similar crowds the world over.

ME: You keep calling her a "sellout." That is not nice. I just did some research and found two interesting pieces of information: 1) 87% of people under the age of 55 have never heard of her; 2) She recorded a song called "Stupid Cupid," which obviously means she hates

Valentine's Day. Interesting. Do you work for her? You are quite militant in your defense of her. (Whoever she is.)

SAL: No, of course I do not work for her. Stupid Cupid was written for her by Neil Sedaka. It was his first million seller. It is true that many of the younger generation have not heard about her. Yet, she has many younger fans. She was a phenomenon in that she was loved by all generations and ethnic groups.

ME: Do you think Connie is good at recognizing satire/sarcasm? It doesn't seem like her fans are.

SAL: She is excellent at it as I am…she is also very witty and as you can see from the article with porn stars, she is very accepting and gracious. She has never looked at stardom or superstardom as anything other than a job and a means of pleasing the public. She had the most extraordinary recording contract in history to date. It just bothers me that someone who should be as recognizable as Elvis is not and it is really her fault, but I don't think it bothers her.

ME: Clearly she is not as good as Elvis. She is probably not even as well known as Paris Hilton. Maybe she should hire that PR firm. What do you think?

SAL: She is as good as Elvis, and not as well known as Paris...and perhaps she should hire her PR firm and then look as simple as Paris does.

ME: If she's as good as Elvis, how come thousands of people don't go to her grave every year on her birthday? Can you explain that?

ME (immediately following the previous email): Time's up. The answer is: Because she is not as good as Elvis. (Or Paris Hilton.)

SAL: Everyone is better than Paris, but I think there is a much better answer than the one you provided. Nevertheless, Elvis is great and so is Connie. During the 60s, Connie was the queen of the Vegas strip and Elvis the king. Now, I have resorted to simpledom in that I am watching Celebrity Fit Club because a local Philly celebrity, Jay McCaroll the first winner of project runway is on the show.

ME: Sorry, I do not correspond with people who watch Celebrity Fit Club. (Whatever that is.) (Though I have heard it is the worst television show in existence and also Jay McCaroll won Project Runway because it was fixed and he is actually from Houston.)

SAL: No, he is not from Houston, but from a small town near The Poconos, PA.

ME: You're probably right, but as we all know, "The Poconos" is Spanish for "Houston."

I never heard from Sal again. It's always sad to lose a friend. I just hope he's doing well. I should also note here that I do not have anything against Connie Francis, which should be obvious because I knew virtually nothing about her before any of this happened. Also, if my house is fire-bombed in the near-future, someone please tell the police to check for leads on the membership list of the fan club for Connie Francis. (Whoever she is.)

~~~

GETTING SOME DISTANCE

With the recent trend of presidential candidates distancing themselves from other people's comments and actions, I came to the conclusion that perhaps I, too, should distance myself from people in my past who have exhibited questionable behavior.

I am not running for anything, but it's probably a good idea, for public consumption, to make it clear that I alone speak and act for myself. Therefore, I have compiled a partial list that should go a long way toward accomplishing that goal.

In high school I knew a guy who insisted that he could put an entire pack of "Red Man" chewing tobacco in his mouth. It turns out he was right. However, when dared to spit the tobacco juice straight up into the air, he took the challenge, but wasn't swift enough to get out of the way. He spent the entire school day with chewing tobacco spit all over his shirt. I wish to distance myself from this person. I had nothing to do with the dare and I did not try the stunt myself. All I did was tell the story to everyone I knew. (And obviously I'm still telling the story, but I am *not* identifying him by name. You're welcome, Keith.)

I hereby distance myself from everyone on the planet who has accused someone else of "comparing apples and oranges." This is one of the worst idioms, not only because it's annoying (all of them are) but also because it makes no sense. Look up the word "compare" and think about the intent of the idiom, which is to imply that two things can't be compared. You'll see what I mean. Furthermore, if you're ever in the vicinity of someone who is actually comparing apples and oranges, leave immediately. There is something wrong with that person.

I was once at a party where a person belched the entire alphabet in French. I wish to distance myself from this person, mainly because he made me feel like an idiot because after two years of taking French the only communication I could achieve in that language was to ask someone: "Did a frog take my luggage to the library?" This is the main reason I haven't gone to France. I was much better at Spanish. I took two years of it and, after all these years, having not spoken very much Spanish, I'm still fairly fluent in the language and would make a great tour guide, as long as you're looking for a taxi or ordering water. Beyond that, you're on your own.

Roughly ten years ago I was involved in a major scandal involving a frozen mouse. A co-worker and I decided we were going to scare our female co-supervisor who was terrified of mice. We didn't have any mice on hand (believe it or not) so we decided to go to a pet store and buy one. It turns out they carried frozen mice only, the idea being that if you owned a snake you could buy the frozen mice, keep them in your freezer, and scare the hell out of someone when they saw the bag of frozen rodents in there and make them think you were a serial killer. Or maybe the idea was to thaw them and feed them to the snake. I can't remember exactly what the salesperson told us because I was laughing too hard the entire time.

Anyway, we bought one frozen mouse (the cashier looked at us in a very odd way) and we returned to work, where we placed the frozen mouse in a room that housed the main server for our computer network. Then we waited. And waited some more. Our intended victim didn't go in there for hours. When we decided to try to get her to go in there, my unnamed co-worker was completely incapable of keeping a straight face and he blew the whole prank in a matter of seconds.

So we were stuck cleaning up the dead mouse, which had thawed and started to secrete some sort of yellowish liquid. I would like to take this time to distance myself from my co-worker because he destroyed a nearly perfect plan. I would also like to distance myself from that disgusting mouse, which did, I should note, receive a proper funeral, by which I mean we shoveled it into a bag and ran it out to the dumpster, making very un-manly noises ("yeeeewwweewww") as we did so. I should also apologize to my former employer, who paid me for that day and so many others like it.

Having publicly admitted guilt in that last story, I would like to take this opportunity to distance myself from myself.

~~~

GOOGLING YOURSELF

Like many people, I have often wondered: What happens if you Google yourself and will it make you go blind? The answer to the first question depends on how common your name is; the answer to the second depends on how often you do it.

I went to Google, typed in my name and found that my blog is the first result. Not surprising, considering that I do not have a particularly common last name, but could I really have that little competition for Internet supremacy from every other Jeff Tompkins in the world? Is our shared name really that…boring?

Here is a sampling of the top "Jeff Tompkins" hits on Google: a lawyer, a realtor, a co-author of a graphic novel called "And I Saw Edgar Allen Poe," a mortgage broker who "specializes in providing home financing to those in the education industry and all those who need it" (in other words, pretty much everyone), and a Recreation and Natural Resource Management Specialist with the United States Department of the Interior. The last one probably explains why my blog frequently gets hits from Google with the search terms "jeff tompkins dc." Whatever a "recreation and natural resource specialist" is, it must be in high demand.

There is a fictional Jeff Tompkins, a character in the 1982 movie *Thou Shalt Not Kill*, played by the actor James Keach, who I've never heard of. But that's OK; I'm sure he's never heard of me, either.

That's not the only Jeff Tompkins associated with the movie industry. Get ready for some excitement here because this one is not fictional. There is a real-life Jeff Tompkins who was a grip for the New Mexico portion of the filming of the 1994 movie "Sleep With Me," which I have never seen so I have no idea how good the gripping was.

Later in my Google search I found this statement, with this exact wording: "Mr. Jeff Tompkins, you are one IGNORANT person, you comments have no bases, I want to know what church you go to and what bible you read?" Upon further investigation I discovered that it was a comment in response to someone named Jeff Tompkins who was urging people to (this is a direct quote) "become a Monotheistic Christian Now, before your natural and eventual death." This fascinating discussion took place in the comments section of a news website called NWI.com, which bills itself as "The Largest and Most Trusted Media Company in Northwest Indiana." I'm sure the other media companies in northwest Indiana are not happy with that kind of arrogance. Be on the lookout for a media turf war in northwest Indiana.

I also found a YouTube video called "A Day in the Life of Jeff Tompkins." If by some chance you ever come across that video, be assured that while it's funny and it looks like something I might have done when I was younger, it isn't me.

You have probably gathered by now that there is just nothing interesting about my name. No one with my name has done anything really noteworthy, either good or bad. And we know this because a simple Google search, using only my name for the search term, proves it. If only there were some way of getting my name on the Internet and associating it with something interesting....

Wait. Why didn't I think of this before?

Jeff Tompkins was a key witness in the Warren Commission report on the assassination of JFK.

Jeff Tompkins, a noted astrophysicist, came up with the idea of putting monkeys in space, not because it was safer than sending humans, but because, hey, come on, monkeys in space!

Jeff Tompkins holds the world record high score for the Atari game "Pitfall."

Jeff Tompkins wrote the script for the final episode of *Cheers*.

Jeff Tompkins, who discovered Babe Ruth and Britney Spears, was Abraham Lincoln's campaign manager.

Jeff Tompkins, future ex-husband of Jennifer Aniston, invented those little plastic packets of soy sauce that come with Chinese food take-out and delivery.

Jeff Tompkins wrote the Pulitzer-Prize winning novel *[Note to editor: Place name of award-winning novel here someday]*.

Jeff Tompkins discovered plutonium, a radioactive element that can be found in old food containers near the back of most bachelors' refrigerators. (Check behind the empty orange juice container.)

Jeff Tompkins is responsible for 15% of the world's peanut butter consumption. Also, 27% of the Pepperidge Farm Goldfish.

Jeff Tompkins never makes up anything or even slightly stretches the truth when he writes.

~~~

MAN VS. PLASTIC

The day started off like most others—roll out of bed and immediately start looking forward to rolling back into it later that night. Breakfast was good, the morning shower was refreshing, and when I got a chance to check outside I saw that the sky had not fallen despite some things I've been hearing on the news lately. But there's still time, I'm told.

After getting some writing done, though, I discovered that this was going to be anything but a "normal" day. My usual practice is to print out some pages that I had written the day before and do some editing. Letting the previous day's work stew a little and then going over it in print provides a valuable and fresh perspective on the words. That is, if you can get the words to appear on the paper. And that requires printer ink, which the cartridge apparently no longer contained. No problem. I had some backup cartridges, purchased at Costco in a multi-pack. It's great to have backups on hand, but only if you can get to them.

The company (which I won't name, but which starts with Hewlett and ends with Packard) apparently has decided that they needed to start packaging these things in human-proof plastic. You have probably come across this type of packing if you've ever been tasked with opening a child's toy on Christmas morning. The material is thick and it appears that some very talented scientists have found a way to weld the plastic ends together.

It quickly became evident that I was going to have to use some kind of tool to get at the cartridges. I spent several minutes fumbling with the edges of this package, trying to create an opening in the seam, but there really was no seam (see: welding). I had not recently been keeping up with my usual hand workout involving ripping phone books in half, so I didn't have the strength to just pull it open.

Scissors seemed like a good idea, but weren't. All I managed to do was place a very small nick in the plastic, and the scissors were starting to bend in a way that I know they're not supposed to, so I gave up and tried something else.

Fire. I had a lighter sitting around and as I went to pick it up it struck me that it was easier to get the lighter out of its package than it was to get to this ink. Are there regulations protecting the public from the dangers of ink cartridges but not from a tool that creates fire, something that actually kills people on a regular basis?

My plan was to melt a small area on the edge of the plastic and while it was still hot and gooey, I'd tear into it. But this plan failed. All I accomplished was the further welding shut of the plastic package. I did manage to fill the room with the scent of burning plastic, but that was not my goal when I got these cartridges.

I was going to have to take extreme measures. I called the aquarium downtown. When the receptionist answered the phone I explained my dilemma and asked her if regular citizens have access to the tanks.

"Why?" she asked.

"I know this is going to sound crazy but I was thinking if you would give me just fifteen minutes, I could dip the package in the water and maybe one of the sharks would nibble it open."

Silence.

"OK, maybe not. Do you have piranhas?"

Click.

Next I called a neighbor to ask if he had anything that might help, like a weed whacker or a chain saw.

"I don't," he said, "but I've had the same problem before. Bring it over. And drive, don't walk."

"Drive?"

"Just do it. We don't have much time," he said, and hung up.

I drove over to his house and he was waiting in the driveway. He walked over and said, "Leave your car running and wait here. Give me the package."

I handed it to him, and he disappeared into his garage for about five minutes. When he emerged, he was holding the package, to which he had attached some vise-grips or clamps or something, one on each end of the package.

"This here is heavy-duty marine rope," he said, holding it up for me to see. "When I was in the Coast Guard we used it for towing distressed boats."

He attached the ropes to each grip, placed the package on the ground and began the task of tying one rope to the front of my car, the other to the back of his. When he completed that, he said, "Back up slowly. Watch me for signals."

I should say here that I detected absolutely no alcohol on his breath. He seemed to be completely sober, and I wondered what it would be like to be around him when he wasn't.

I put the car in reverse, keeping an eye on his hand, which was making a motion indicating that I should keep going. "Give her a little gas," he instructed. I followed the order. I couldn't see what was happening to the package but a grin slowly grew across his face so I assumed it was going well.

"Now STOP!" He put his hand higher in the air, giving me what I assumed was the "halt" signal, but his yelling for me to stop did the trick.

He bent down and came back up holding the package in his hand, which was now open, with the two pieces hinged at the bottom like a freshly steamed clam.

He gave me the cartridges, tipped his hat and said, "Go forth and print."

Since that day I have been thinking about my neighbor's remarkable ingenuity. I keep wondering what made him come up with that idea, and how many times he has drawn and quartered items encased in impenetrable plastic. Or people. There's a rumor, but I can't go into it here.

~~~

JEFF TOMPKINS

ODD JOB

I have been trying to identify the most ludicrous occupation in the world and I think I may have located it. I do not mean to imply that I researched every occupation in the world. That endeavor would qualify as the winner, and the process would be moot. Unless I got a huge government grant for the study, which, now that I think about it, might actually be possible. That is, if there's any government grant money left after studying the mating habits of giraffes and the grooming techniques of the yak. But I digress.

My study took place over the course of many years and consisted of observing jobs in person—sometimes my own, when I was actually paying attention to what I was doing, which was rarely necessary in most of my jobs—and some observed on a third-party basis, such as watching others perform their jobs on TV.

One of my first jobs was through a "temp service," which is code for a company hiring you without having to give you benefits. The job was about thirty minutes from home and while the time spent in the car would be an annoyance, the travel cost wasn't a hindrance because this was back when you could afford a full tank of gas without having to sell a major bodily organ. When I arrived at the job I was told that I would be organizing a warehouse, which didn't sound good, and wasn't, because it involved operating a forklift. The people at the temp service had, for some reason, failed to ask me if I knew how to operate a forklift, which I didn't. I don't think I had even been near a forklift, except for some instances of trivial vandalism when I was much younger. So long ago, in fact, that the statute of limitations has long expired, which is why I'm free to mention it here.

Anyway, I listened intently to the warehouse manager's instructions and thirty minutes later, when everything had been explained to me, when I was ready to get into the forklift and get to work, when the manager went to another part of the building to do something, I promptly located the nearest door, slipped out, and went home.

I'm not saying that my job (or what was *supposed to be* my job) was stupid. I'm saying the occupation of temp service job placement is. How else could you explain the fact that they subjected me to roughly two hours of personality tests and computer proficiency exams for a forklift job? Now, I'm not an expert in job placement, but it seems to me that if you're hiring someone to drive a forklift, the test should be: Can this person drive a forklift?

There are many jobs that remain a mystery to me. For instance, any kind of professional "critic." The way I see it, we're all movie critics, food critics, book critics, etc. The only difference between us and the professional critics is that we don't get paid to express our opinions. Maybe there's a special kind of pretense that we—the common herd, non-wine-swishing types who like movies that actually make money—just don't possess.

(Ironic note: I got paid to write that last paragraph in which I critiqued the critics.)

Now we arrive at the announcement of the most preposterous job in the world. The decision wasn't an easy one, especially considering the fact that I had "tech support" and "help desk" on the list. But without further delay, I announce that the most ludicrous job in the universe is: symphony conductor.

Here's a person who stands in front of dozens of people who are actually playing the music, and all he has to do is make dramatic gestures and wave a little stick around. I'm aware of the possibility that someone is going to read this and claim that the symphony needs "the maestro" in order for the music to hold its continuity. At least, that's what I read somewhere on the Internet where someone was explaining the job of the conductor.

In response, I would first point out that the word "maestro" is Italian for "master," and implies genius or rare talent. What kind of genius or rare talent is required to gesticulate with a chopstick? And secondly, are we to believe that if the maestro put down the stick and walked off the stage that the members of the symphony, all of whom are alleged trained musicians, would suddenly not know what to do? Would they start playing random notes and wind up sounding like a herd of elephants with upper respiratory infections?

I just don't buy it. But what do I know? I can't even drive a forklift.

~~~

TRANSCRIPT OF NEGOTIATIONS BETWEEN U.S. NAVY AND SOMALI PIRATES

Now that Captain Richard Phillips has been rescued by the U.S. Navy, the Defense Department has declassified a transcript of communications between the U.S.S. Bainbridge and the Somali pirates who were holding Phillips captive aboard a lifeboat.

NAVY HOSTAGE NEGOTIATOR: This is the United States Navy. Are you prepared to negotiate?

LEAD PIRATE: Yes. We want one million dollars.

NAVY: Sorry, that's not going to happen.

PIRATE: Okay, then two million.

NAVY: What we mean is that we don't pay ransom.

PIRATE: Oh.

NAVY: Plus, when you're negotiating and your first demand is rejected, your second demand should be lower.

PIRATE: Thanks, we'll remember that next time. That is very helpful.

NAVY: Our pleasure. Last week we were able to help some other pirates save a ton of money by switching to—

PIRATE: Geico. We know that joke.

NAVY: Damn. Anyway, we are here to help.

PIRATE: Is that why you have those large guns pointed at us?

NAVY: We'll get to that later. *(Laughter in the background.)* Tell us what you want. We'd like to get

Captain Phillips released safely.

PIRATE: We have discussed it among ourselves and we have a list of demands.

NAVY: Proceed.

PIRATE: Arrrrrr. Bring me one noggin of rum, now, won't you, matey?

NAVY: Come again?

PIRATE: We are pirates! That is how pirates talk.

NAVY: Fine. Just get on with the demands, please. We'd like to resolve this in time to see the final round of The Masters.

PIRATE: We want the following items: A parrot, three eye-patches, three fake hooks that we can attach to our hands, three bandannas, three swords, three pairs of baggy pants that are held up by tying scarves around the waist, three of those skull-and-crossbones flags—

NAVY: Hold it. You're just naming a bunch of pirate stereotypes. What's next, three peg-legs?

PIRATE: *(Mumbling as the three pirates talk it over.)*

NAVY: Hello?

PIRATE: Yes, yes, peg-legs. We forgot about that one. Add it to the list.

NAVY: Why only one parrot but three of everything else?

PIRATE: It is not easy to find three parrots this far out in the ocean.

NAVY: Well, we don't even have one parrot and in fact we don't have any of these items aboard our ship. It would probably take several days to get all of those items out here.

PIRATE: Shiver me timbers!

NAVY: What? What happened?

PIRATE: I am talking like a pirate again to reinforce the image that I am a pirate.

NAVY: Are you sure you aren't doing it just because it's in the dialogue?

PIRATE: Yes, you got me. Who wrote this script, anyway?

NAVY: We have no idea. Probably some blogger who thought he would try to work in all the pirate stuff he could think of without looking it up on Google, just so he could post it while the idea was fresh in his mind even if he wasn't sure how to wrap it up, but we do have reliable intelligence indicating that this is probably going to end with a very well-known pirate cliché.

PIRATE: Ha! I laugh in his face. How predictable! If this were real, I'd make him walk the plank.

NAVY: We knew it.

~~~

WE AREN'T THE CHAMPIONS

If there is one thing we Americans love, other than deep-fried food, it's competition. It's the basis of our civilization. We live by the cherished ideal that if two or more people are locked in a battle for first place—whether it's sports, business or *American Idol*—and one person puts in the hard work and dedication that makes them the best, then we, as a society, recognize everyone else as a worthless loser.

The point here is that competition is good, at least for the people who are doing the actual competing. Spectators exist merely to fund the competition and respond with the mandatory misappropriated glee when their side wins, and unwarranted suicidal tendencies when their side loses. These behaviors can be observed in every sports venue in this country. We have to win. Well, they, the actual competitors, have to win, and we have to feel like we won because we wanted the winner to win, and need to feel that we defeated the other side because we wanted them to lose. Or something psychological like that.

Speaking of "we," who exactly is the "we" in phrases like "We need to get this first down," or "We should have hit that basket before the half"? These comments are often heard in living rooms and bars, where people are watching the game on TV, swilling beer and stuffing their faces with chips and dip. If you don't have a uniform on, you're not "we." And wearing a jersey doesn't count.

This "we" phenomenon seems to be unique to sports fans. For instance, if someone is talking about the Grammys and the award for Song of the Year went to their favorite band, the person never says, "We won!" Or, if they're talking about their favorite movie being nominated for an Academy Award for Best Picture, the person never says, "We're gonna get that Oscar. It's ours! We can do this!" Why don't they? They contributed money by purchasing CDs, DVDs, tickets, t-shirts, etc., just like sports fans, and surely they provided some vital clapping and cheering.

Maybe they're just not as earnest as sports fans, many of whom take fandom so seriously that they resort to violence to express themselves. What's interesting is that you can't always tell if this aggression is an outpouring of glee or disappointment. When you see a sports riot, with people clogging city streets, burning couches, smashing windows and assaulting police horses, it is sometimes difficult to tell if they're the winning fans or the losing fans.

I bring all this up, first, because it has bugged me for several years, and, secondly, because now that college football has crowned its alleged national champion, and the NFL has wrapped up for the season, we are closing in on that time of the year when the nation turns its lonely eyes to a completely different kind of competition. I am of course talking about the Southeastern Beard and Moustache Championships. Yes, this is an actual event.

One website said this competition "attracts facial hair enthusiasts from all parts of the country and their devoted fans." See what I mean? There are even fans for beards and moustaches. We Americans will accept any kind of competition people can think up, which explains why some people will watch cars drive around in circles for hours and hours and hours and why they (the people, not the cars) go into great detail about how fast someone changed a tire.

But back to this beard and moustache competition. It was scheduled to take place last Saturday, but I can find no information about it, such as who won or whether it even took place, considering that we had a snowstorm here the night before. Perhaps it was canceled or rescheduled, which might be good if there had been a category for length, but I don't think there was. The site listed the following categories: sideburns, goatee, moustache, recession beard, full beard freestyle, ladies artificial, gray beard & full beard. (Notice there is a category for "ladies artificial," but not "ladies natural.")

Obviously this is not a competition where you can watch someone's beard and/or moustache grow. That would be boring, and that's what golf is for. So it's probably more like a dog show, where judges rank the facial hair based on grooming or luster or some other criteria. Maybe they give points to the beard or moustache that contains the fewest pieces of food. Or maybe the most pieces.

I'll try to find out if the competition has been rescheduled or if we have to wait until next year for the second annual Southeastern Beard and Moustache Championships. Either way, what you as a fan need to do is pick a competitor to root for. Purchase a replica of that guy's (or lady's) jersey, some bumper stickers and a big "We're #1" foam-beard and get ready. "You" might win, and you certainly wouldn't want to be caught in that situation without the proper ways to rub the losing fans' faces in it, would you?

Lastly, let me say to all the serious sports fans out there who might not like what I've said in this article: Please do not to come to my house and drag my couch out onto the lawn and burn it. Thank you.

~~~

THESE KIDS TODAY

I had always hoped I'd never become one of those people who reaches a certain age and starts saying things like, "These kids today, I swear." I'm sorry to announce that I have become such a person.

It's not the usual things like pointing out that their music consists of loud noise and indiscernible lyrics, or fretting over the way they wear their pants halfway down their buttocks, flagrantly disregarding the "under" in "underwear." Mine is a complaint based on the sociological fact that today's kids possess a level of common sense usually found in the mollusk family.

As proof, I point to the online how-to manual called Wikihow.com, specifically an article titled: "How To Give Your Friends Your Phone Number."

Here is a summary of the article, complete with actual quotes:

—Tell friends your phone number. Now, who would have ever thought of that! They also warn that you should be cautious, because someone you might not want to have your phone number may overhear it. Therefore: *"You may also write your phone number on a piece of paper to give to all of your friends. However, also make sure that somebody who you don't want calling you reads it or finds it."* This is good training for kids who are considering a career with the CIA.

—Send your friends an email, and: *"Write in the email what your home phone number is."* Apparently, the authors of this article discovered that kids were sending each other blank emails.

—Add your number to your friends' cell phones. *"Ask before you do this, though."* In other words, don't steal your friends' cell phones and alter their contacts. (Unless you're training for a career with the CIA.)

—Send your friends a post-card with your phone number on it. This seems to violate the privacy measure urged in Suggestion One, but that's not the worst of it. The article adds: *"Make sure you know your friend's address, though, before doing this."* Excellent point. We would not want to clog up the U.S. Postal Service with millions of post-cards containing nothing but phone numbers, addressed to no one in particular. They might fall into the hands of unscrupulous telemarketers.

—Remind friends what your phone number is. *"Tell them throughout the day if you don't want them to forget. Write your phone number on their hand if it is alright with them."* The warning against writing on someone's body without their permission is very insightful, but this stipulation they included should not be ignored: *"Don't keep telling your friends what your phone number is, or else they could get annoyed. If they already know your home phone number, there is no use in just going around reminding them all of the time."* The authors apparently don't have the heart to tell the kids that if you have to keep reminding someone what your phone number is, chances are they were never going to call in the first place.

In the spirit of this article, and considering the apparent problem of today's kids not knowing how to accomplish the most basic everyday tasks, I figured I would contribute to the longstanding social tradition of passing along crucial information to the next generation.

If you're going to eat things such as soup or cereal, use a spoon instead of a fork. Also, remember to hold the spoon with the concave side facing up. If you do not know what "concave" means, ask your science teacher.

If you want to write something permanently on a piece of paper, use a pen instead of a pencil. Also, remember to take the cap off the pen first.

If you would like to go to a friend's house, the best ways to get there are: walking; running; riding a bike or skateboard; riding in a car driven by your parents, or your friend's parents, but not a random person who drives up slowly to the curb and offers you a ride and free candy. Also, do not try to ride your dog over there.

When bathing or showering, remove your clothes first. Remember, shoes off before socks.

Blinking your eyelids is handled automatically by your brain. You do not have to worry about this. However, in the unlikely event that you notice that you're suddenly in the dark, even though you're outside on a sunny day, it's possible that you forgot to move your eyelids up after moving them down. Simply use the muscles that control your eyelids to reopen your eyes.

It is best to chew thoroughly before swallowing. This aids in the digestion process and also reduces the risk of choking. Remember to insert the food into your mouth before chewing.

When selecting something to watch on TV, it is best to sit facing the screen, so you can enjoy the visual as well as the audio portion of the broadcast. Otherwise, the TV is, well, pretty much just a radio.

Those are just a few practical ideas that should be useful to current children. There's one more that I should include: If you're a kid reading this, be advised that you have reached the end of this column. STOP READING HERE.

~~~

HOW MAY I HELP YOU VERY MUCH?

Sometimes people ask me to help them with their computers. (These are almost always people I know; rarely do strangers ask me.) I suppose it's my fault, as I have apparently given people the impression that I know what I'm doing when it comes to these machines.

While I probably know as much as the average person, I certainly don't know as much as our local "Computer Guy" on Comcast channel 2, Jamey Mellis. I also don't know as much as the people at "tech support." You know—the people you call who are in a time zone so far away that it's a completely different day; the same ones who answer the phone by saying, "How may I help you very much?"

Many years ago when I first started to use computers, they were so primitive that they would malfunction, on average, every five or six minutes. Sometimes I would see an error that said "SYNTAX ERROR IN LINE 323" or "RUN DLL ERROR" or "YOU CAN'T CLICK ON THAT, YOU MORON."

At that point, I would employ the highly effective Computer Repair Alternative Procedure (C.R.A.P.) that called for the user to hold down the CTRL and ALT keys and bang on the side of the monitor until the frustration subsided. Surprisingly, this rarely worked, at least not right away. I would usually turn off the computer and come back an hour or two days later and it worked fine.

But these days computers seem to malfunction less frequently. For instance, right now I'm typing on my laptop and there is not the slightest hint of any probl^(*L,#. Everything is working fine.

However, should something go wrong, I will probably be able to fix it due to the fact that I'm now more advanced in my computer knowledge than I was in those ancient days of Windows 95 and the C.R.A.P. method—the days when the Internet was new…and very slow…when "www" meant "wait, wait, wait" and you could go out for ice cream and come back before the entire page loaded.

Now, with over a decade of computer experience, I know that I can't just bang on the side of the monitor. Mainly this is due to the fact that laptops have thin monitors so you really can't bang on the side of it. It wouldn't provide that stress-relieving *bang!* that the old monitors did. And they call this progress?

I now have all new ways of dealing with problems, some of which you probably use if you, like me, are only somewhat knowledgeable about computers.

For instance, if you're trying to start a program and it doesn't immediately appear on the screen, there's no need to wait forever for it to start. Just keep clicking (*click-click-clickclickclickclick...*) many times, in rapid succession. Do not stop until the program loads or until you see a small puff of smoke emerge from the speakers, whichever comes first. Note: It may be necessary, from a technical standpoint, to utter several curse words.

If you should ever experience what computer experts call "freezing," wherein the computer stops functioning and the keyboard and mouse don't work, there is no need to call tech support. They're only going to tell you that you need to do a "hard restart" to reboot the computer. This means that instead of restarting your computer the usual way (by clicking on the Start button and then clicking on Restart) you hold down the power button, really hard (hence the "hard restart"), similar to the way you would press down hard with your shoe on a roach or a hairy, multi-colored spider. Again, it would probably help to curse at this point and because the computer is rebooting you will have plenty of time for this task, so here's a helpful list of things to curse: your computer, computers in general, the manufacturer of your computer, the person who invented computers, the person who sold you the computer and/or the person who delivered the computer to your house, Bill Gates and Microsoft, and (hey, why not?) the IRS.

Sometimes you may notice that your computer is running very slow, beginning with the startup process and including attempts to open various applications. This could be an indication that your computer has become infected with a virus. The best way to deal with a virus is to make sure that your computer takes in plenty of fluids and rests for a few days. Just let it run its course. Feel free to try cursing as well.

As you can see from the advice in this article, I am quite knowledgeable about computers. If you have any problems, just give me a call. If I do not answer, please leave a message—your call is very important. If I'm here, I promise not to answer by asking if I can help you very much.

~~~

MUST SEE TV? I'LL BE THE JUDGE

I have good news for The American People: If you think TV is bad now, hang in there just a little longer. In a few weeks, I will have a say in what should and should not be on TV. That's right—I will be a Nielsen Family.

Contrary to popular myth, this does not mean that I have to change my last name to Nielsen. In fact, the rules are so lax that I do not even have to get a family. That's good news, because this is short notice and currently my household family consists of me and a few bugs that do not pay rent and come and go at all hours like unruly teenagers. I have control over nothing.

When the call came, the lady on the other end of the line told me I had been selected to participate in the Nielsen ratings. Apparently, there is a rigorous selection process whereby someone in a call-center dials a random number and if a live human answers they say, "Congratulations! We know hardly anyone watches the mindless drivel on TV these days, so in order to make it more enjoyable, we are giving you an exclusive opportunity to watch the drivel and write things down! Doesn't that sound great? Hello?"

I suspect that when most people get this call, they hang up and resume whatever entertaining thing they were going, such as staring at the wall. But I stayed on the line, in part because despite having written for the Nielsen group before, I had no idea how their process worked and I wanted to find out. This is something I probably should have looked into before I wrote for them, but in keeping with today's journalistic standards, I did absolutely no research.

The other reason I didn't hang up was that there was nothing good on TV at that moment, so the call had the potential to be a better form of entertainment.

If you have declined to participate in the Nielsen ratings research, I'm sorry to inform you that you missed out on something. I'm not talking about the chance to influence the course of TV programming; I'm talking about the pay. Yes, they pay people to watch TV. A dream job! Well, it would be a dream job, if there were any good shows left. But there aren't and that's okay, considering the fact that the pay is five entire dollars. I would guess that in the current economic situation, that could very well bump some people up to a higher tax bracket.

During the call I was told I will be receiving some kind of booklet and I'm supposed to use it to do something with something. I'm not quite sure. I've never been really good at following directions. I don't think I have an attention problem, though. It's more of a problem with authority.

For instance, I have been known to buck the system by not following the warning label on electronic devices that says: WARN CHILDREN OF THE RISK OF INJURY OR DEATH BY ELECTRIC SHOCK. I have no children, so what am I supposed to do? Find one and start talking to them about it? I wouldn't be comfortable doing that.

Anyway, I'll figure out the booklet when I get it. No need to worry about that now, because I've been coming up with ways to make an impact on TV programming.

First, I'm going to try to find a way to put an end to all sports interviews. They are pointless. If you're a football coach or player, for example, you're going to tell us that you're hoping the defense doesn't give up big plays, the offense executes and blocks "good" (not "well"; this is sports, after all) and that your special teams don't make any mistakes. This sounded profound when I was seven years old, but it doesn't anymore. We get it. You want to play "good" and you hope the other team plays "bad."

Second, I will make a valiant effort to remove all programming involving Donald Trump.

Third, I have no idea if I'll be asked about commercials but I intend to write about it in the booklet even if they tell me not to. The major thing that needs changing is the frequency with which strangers appear on our TVs and solemnly confess appalling facts about their bowels. We, the public, have put up with this long enough.

If you have been selected to be a Nielsen Family, I hope you will use this opportunity to make a difference. Your country is counting on you.

If you haven't been selected, feel free to contact me and let me know if there's anything you'd like to change on TV. (I charge only $5 for this, apparently.)

If you think everything is just fine with TV programming these days, we'll disagree, but I think your voice should be heard, too. And as proof of my civility I say: Get your own damn booklet.

~~~

SURVIVAL CAN BE A BEAR

Finally, there's a program on television from which we all can learn valuable information. You know how it is when you're dropped from a helicopter in the middle of the Rocky Mountains and you have to find your way out while avoiding grizzly bears? Or when you find yourself lost in the middle of the Moab Desert in 100-degree heat with no water? Or how about the time you were abandoned in Alaska's Chugach Mountains, forced to find your way to civilization by making your way down a 200-foot waterfall and eating raw salmon for a few days?

What you could have used were the skills of the host of The Discovery Channel's *Man vs. Wild*. His name is Bear Grylls, which is pronounced "bear grills." This is not to be confused with any of the survival techniques on the show. Makers of "bear grills" advise that you should only grill bears in your backyard. You should never haul the grill out into the wilderness to find a bear for grilling. (The legal department told me to include that statement.)

The point of this show is to teach us average city-slickers how to survive potentially life-threatening situations should we find ourselves stranded in an exotic location populated with fauna (and in some cases, flora) that could kill us.

In one episode, Grylls arrives via parachute in Costa Rica's Osa Peninsula rain forest, to face poisonous snakes, vicious mosquitoes and deadly river currents. Now that sounds like a nice vacation destination! But I'm going to take a wild guess and assume that that description won't be appearing on any Costa Rica rain forest travel brochures.

The description for episode two, season two, in which Grylls is in Iceland, says: "Because finding food is a problem in this [arctic] climate, Bear is forced to eat a sheep's eyeball." Really? He was forced? Where was the rest of the sheep—namely, the part that resembles, I don't know…a lamb chop? Did he just happen to stumble upon an abandoned sheep eyeball? And if so, what exactly is going on in Iceland? I'm going to assume that Grylls's brain was frostbitten, because that's what it would take for me to eat the eyeball of an animal that contains parts that resemble food you can buy at the grocery store.

A commercial for season two shows Grylls eating a grub (defined by the dictionary as: short, fat, worm-like larva, especially of beetles) while the voice-over says, "Does Bear Grylls really need to do these things? Probably not. But you might!" Putting aside the fact that that sounds like some kind of threat, I'm assuming that if this guy gets paid for doing something he "probably" doesn't need to do, there's no chance I'm going to do it for free. But thanks, anyway.

Another episode features our wilderness hero explaining why drinking your own urine could save your life. This seems like the most appropriate situation for that famous television disclaimer: DO NOT TRY THIS AT HOME. SERIOUSLY. DON'T DRINK PEE. WE'RE NOT KIDDING.

Even if Bear Grylls has a good reason for drinking urine, there's still the nagging question of whether we should be taking culinary advice from a guy who ate a sheep's eyeball. Now, I know that in some cultures, imbibing urine is perfectly acceptable. And I wouldn't even be surprised if these cultures had "urine snobs," much like we in the West have "wine snobs." They probably slosh the urine around in a glass, sniff it, and make comments like: "This definitely does not have a fruity aroma, but I'm getting a hint of salt." (Hey, don't blame me for talking about this. The other guy *drank* the stuff. At least he got *paid* to do it…even though he "probably" didn't need to.)

Maybe I'm being a little harsh on Mr. Grylls. Maybe he really is helping people survive. I would have no way of knowing just how difficult the wild can be, considering the fact that the closest I've come to "the wild" in my adult life was the time we lost power for three days after an ice storm. Conditions were harsh: no microwave, no TV, no computer (after the laptop battery lost its charge). It was man against nature. I had to go all the way to the back porch to cook a London broil and assorted vegetables on the grill. Luckily, I made it back inside, where the temperature (I am not kidding here) was 45 degrees.

One survival skill I could have used at that time was how to warm up a toilet seat. I bet Bear Grylls, in all of his outdoor quests, has never had to sit on a toilet seat that has been exposed to 40-something temps for a few days.

~~~

JEFF TOMPKINS

WHAT'S IN A NAME? AND WHAT'S YOUR NAME AGAIN?

Recently I was reading a blog where people were discussing differences between men and women. As you can imagine, this was a very long discussion. Men were listing things that they didn't understand about women. Women were listing things they didn't understand about men. Women were responding to the men. Men just kept on listing things. Women realized that the men were not paying attention and added "men don't pay attention" to the list. But very few of us men noticed it.

A particularly nasty exchange occurred when the women pointed out that not only do men not listen to women when they're telling a story, sometimes men aren't listening even when women are imparting vital information such as their name.

According to these women, this happens a lot. And these particular women indicated that it would be much better if the man would simply tell the truth and ask the woman to repeat her name. But, they said, men never do this; men come up with other ways of finding out a woman's name.

There is a *Seinfeld* episode that deals with this sociological predicament. At one point the woman tells Jerry that he's sweet and says, "Oh, Jerry," and hugs him. Jerry, having no idea what her name is, responds, "Oh…*you*."

The fictitious TV character woman didn't pick up on it, but apparently women in real life would, if the women contributing to the blog are telling the truth. "I would have known right there!" claimed one. "Who calls people 'you'? That would have been a red flag for me."

If you've seen that episode of *Seinfeld* ("The Junior Mints") you know that things didn't turn out well for Jerry. But that's only because he wasn't creative. He didn't even try. All he had to do was something that I heard about…read about…a friend of mine once…

OK, I admit it! It was me. I'm guilty. It happened many years ago, at a party, and what I did was this:

I claimed that I was taking psychology class and told what's-her-name that one thing we learned in class was that you can tell a lot about a person from their handwriting. So I asked her to write something on a napkin—"It doesn't have to be long, you can just write your name"—and she went along with it. I picked up the napkin, saw what her name was, and then launched into a huge load of bull about handwriting analysis, what it means if a person links certain letters together, what it means if they print in all CAPS, etc.

Then a slight panic: What if she knew what I was up to and she wrote down the wrong name, on purpose, hoping I would call her that name and she'd bust me?

Then I relaxed a little, having realized that I could blame it all on her by reminding her that she's the one who wrote down the wrong name. "Ha!" I would say indignantly. "You *lied* to me!" But it turns out she wrote down her real name.

Which I can't remember right now. But that's not the point. And while it's true that my scheme wouldn't have worked outside the presence of alcohol, that isn't the point, either.

The point, of course, is that if you're a guy and you've just met a woman and you're trying to make a good first impression, one thing you absolutely cannot do is tell her the truth. Now, most guys will apply that standard to nearly every part of the conversation, but for legal reasons I'm advocating it only in the unfortunate event that you forget the woman's name. There's no way you can say, "I know we've been having this discussion for a while now and you've spent a good part of your evening getting to know me and allowing me to get to know you, but one thing I'd really like to know is, what's your name again?"

You have to come up with a way to find out her name without her finding out what you're trying to find out. Sometimes guys are good at this, sometimes they aren't. And sometimes, let's admit it, guys come up with an idea that is pure genius.

Who do you think came up with the idea for those stickers that say: "HELLO, MY NAME IS _____"?

~~~

STUFF IT

It's time for Thanksgiving, a holiday in which we gather together with loved ones to give thanks for the blessings in life, such as owning a new fast laptop and being a fan of a college football team that has a pretty good shot at the conference championship. You know, important things like that.

But this is also a holiday that is very good for people of my gender (which, by the way, is male) because this holiday doesn't involve gifts. We guys don't have to wander around malls looking for something special for that someone special. Sometimes this wandering can go on for days. You know how sometimes you drive by a mall that is closed and you see cars in the parking lot? Those are not abandoned cars; those are cars with guys sleeping in them, guys who were unable to find the Perfect Gift for their significant other, guys who figured that rather than go home they might as well stay right there at the mall overnight so they can get a head-start the next morning.

I have just painted a rather bleak picture of the average male's ability to pick out the Perfect Gift, but I would remind you ladies reading this that it is *not* our fault. You should just come right out and tell us some things you'd like to have, or drop hints, and don't make it too subtle. For instance, if you're hoping to receive something, we advise you to find a picture of it, print out roughly 12,000 copies and leave them around where we will eventually notice. (WARNING: I cannot guarantee that this method will work with all guys; there are some guys who are likely to put the picture in an envelope and give it to you. Know your situation.)

But back to Thanksgiving. We guys really like this holiday because it involves three things that stir our deepest emotions: eating, football and naps. We get to eat food that we don't have to (or can't) cook, and then we get to slink off to the den and fall into comfortable chairs and turn on the game, which we won't see much of because we fall asleep due to seriously high levels of tryptophan running through our system. We swear, were it not for this temporary medical condition, we would clear the table and wash the dishes, silverware, pots and pans. It's a shame that the American Medical Association advises against this, but what can you do?

Now, this all sounds very good (to guys, at least) but Thanksgiving is not without its hazards. That's what I found out when I Googled the keywords "Thanksgiving safety." I did that because of this culture's trend toward irrational alarmism, and sure enough there were several articles detailing the various ways in which your Thanksgiving can become an emergency situation.

For example, most of the articles listed choking as the number one Thanksgiving danger, pointing out that while this is most common in children and the elderly, anyone can get something stuck in their throat once the booze gets flowing. Other dangers include: cutting yourself while slicing turkey and lighting the kitchen on fire. As you know if you're a regular reader, I like to pass along helpful tips to people, so I would advise that you take great caution when deciding where to have Thanksgiving. If you think there is a chance that you will end up at someone's house where drunk people are choking on wishbones while someone is in another room bleeding out from a knife mishap, and while others are trying to put out a kitchen fire, do not go to that house. It's just not worth it.

I also found a website that listed Thanksgiving safety tips for birds. It's true. It took me a moment to realize that these safety tips do not apply to all birds (such as…oh, I don't know…let's say turkeys) but rather to pet birds. They told the story of a cockatiel named Charlie who accidentally landed in pot of boiling water and ended up having to wear bandages on his legs for a while. They didn't come right out and say so, but I got the impression that boiled cockatiel is not good. They also mention that birds are very susceptible to stress and advise that you put your bird in a cage, alone, in a secure area of your home until all the guests have left. They didn't have the guts to say it, but I will: That also works well with children.

So we see that Thanksgiving can be an enjoyable time but also a dangerous one. And I didn't even mention the morning after, the official start of the Christmas season, when people line up outside stores at 4 a.m. to get good deals and trample one another. 'Tis the season....

~~~

TALKING SMALL

I read a lot about writers, particularly writers of fiction, and one piece of advice that I see in every book, magazine, and blog is: Listen to real life conversations so your dialogue sounds like real people.

When dialogue is done well, the characters have more credibility because they seem real. When done badly, dialogue can ruin a character and, by extension, the entire story. Let's explore some examples of good and bad dialogue. For this scene, let's assume a guy has run into a friend on the day of a concert...

GOOD DIALOGUE: "What's up? You coming with us to the show tonight?"

BAD DIALOGUE: "Hello, Jonathon. I am wondering if you have yet decided as to whether or not you will be accompanying us to the concert this evening, Jonathon."

Obviously the first example sounds real. You can picture the guys standing in a Stop-N-Go or something, buying beer (probably in the middle of a weekday, but forget about that for now). The second example, however, just doesn't sound real. Nobody talks like that. Well, no one outside of Great Britain, at least. And no one uses the other person's name that frequently, unless they're trying to sell something.

So dialogue is important. And, yes, it seems to make sense that you would learn to write better dialogue by listening to actual people engaging in some actual conversations. The problem, though, is that most real life dialogue is boring.

If you've ever stood in line behind two people who haven't seen each other recently, you know exactly what I'm talking about. These people will discuss the most mundane issues imaginable.

Hey, long time no see. Hey, there! How are things going? Good, good...you? Great. How's the family? Great. Christie is in cheerleading camp all week so Sarah and I have the house to ourselves. How about you? Well, you know, just working and trying to stay ahead. Joanne finally decided what color she wanted to paint the bathroom so we're going to tackle that this weekend. Hey, whatever happened to that tree problem you were having? Oh, we had that taken care of. The guy said it was some kind of fungus…

On and on these two people will go, neither really caring what the other says. One is thinking that he'd really like it if this line hurried up so he could get in his car and get home. The other is thinking: I can't even remember this guy's name but I think he knows my wife or our wives know each other and we met at a Christmas party two years ago. And the cashier is thinking: If I hear one more conversation like this, I'm going to grab someone by the neck and drag them across this conveyer belt.

Another major real life small talk topic is the ever exciting discussion about the weather. *Beautiful day, huh? Yeah, sure is. I think it's supposed to get warmer tomorrow. Oh good, I hadn't heard that. But we could use a little rain. Tell me about it. I can't remember the last time we had rain. We had a little last week, or was it the week before? I don't know, but my sprinkler sure is getting a workout.*

Nobody wants to read dialogue like that in a novel. You probably didn't even want to read it in this article. I had trouble staying awake just writing it. But for some reason, people are entertained by this type of drivel. So would *they* read a book where everyone just engaged in small talk? Maybe there's a huge market out there waiting for such a novel. A market of small talkers. Of course, if someone were to write the book, they would only sell one copy because the chronic small talkers would spoil it for everyone else.

Two people standing in a grocery store (blocking the aisle, of course): *Hey, so good to see you! It's been too long. I think the last time we saw each other was at Mary's, right? No, I think it was at the pool. Oh yeah, I forgot about that. How could I forget about that? So what's new? The kids are doing great; we're just having some trouble adjusting to the time change. It's a real bear trying to get them up for school this week. What about you? Well, I'm reading this great book called "Talking Small" and I think you would love it! What's it about? People who talk and talk and talk and never exchange any meaningful information. Ha ha ha, I can't STAND people like that, but, hey, can you believe how expensive rice is now?*

~~~

WEATHER ADVISORY

I generally believe that technology is a good thing; the more of it the better. When it comes to weather forecasting, however, I have my doubts. It appears that much of the live weather coverage has become more about showcasing computer graphics than covering the actual weather that is going on outside your actual house in the actual "real world" that exists outside the *Storm Center Super Weather Lab 24/7 Theater of Nervousness 5,000.*

"As you can see from this line of blue arrows here on the screen, there are several blue arrows in the area."

"If you look closely here, you'll see this rotating column. That indicates the presence of a tornado. Or possibly the absence of one. Or it could be something our new weather software does that I'm not familiar with because I haven't finished the tutorial yet. But take cover NOW!"

"We are getting reports of debris on the ground. Live Weather Extreme Tracker 6.0 Ultimate is not picking this up yet, but we just had a viewer call in who told our producer that there is a medium-size twig on the ground near his driveway. We have a crew on the way."

I'm not saying that we should ignore weather alerts. I'm saying that we probably don't need four-hour marathon coverage of the storms. Just give us the scrolling messages like you used to.

As annoying as they are, I'd rather see that on the screen than a couple of meteorologists with their sleeves rolled up, sweating and panting, as though they're reporting a nuclear explosion in the harbor. Save it for the big one. Like a hurricane. Speaking of hurricanes....

Yesterday's *Post & Courier* (Charleston, S.C.) reported that the National Weather Service office in North Carolina issued the season's first hurricane warning:

According to the advisory, a tropical storm was about 150 miles off the coast from Charleston and was expected to make landfall today as a Category 1 hurricane.

You might be thinking that the big problem here is that residents were caught off-guard, totally unprepared for this tropical event. And you would be wrong. The big problem is that there was *no hurricane*.

Nothing even close to it. How did this happen? (This is a complete shocker, so get ready.) It was a malfunction of weather forecasting software.

So we aren't going to have a hurricane. But what will happen?

Here is my forecast: 78 degrees, clear and sunny, with a 90% chance of hurricanes, landslides, or perfect boating weather. Tonight will be cloudy with heavy rain and/or clear skies. After nightfall, there is a 70% chance of darkness.

~~~

JEFF TOMPKINS

TWENTY

Recently a friend reminded me that our 20-year high-school reunion is coming up. My reaction was: Hmmm. Twenty years? It seems like just yesterday I was experiencing a lack of confidence when talking to girls and coming up with creative excuses for not doing what I was supposed to be doing. Wait. That *was* yesterday. Some things never change.

Anyway, it got me thinking about those old times. A faint memory will pop into my head and I'll spend a few minutes wondering what a certain person's name was, or what year it might have happened, who I was dating at the time, etc. Many of those questions go unanswered, probably due to the fact that I've spent the better part of the last twenty years trying to forget everything that happened in high school.

OK, maybe not everything. I'll never forget the time my locker-mate brought a pistol to school with the intention of shooting his girlfriend. After he was caught walking around with the gun (before he could shoot anyone) the police wanted to search our locker for more evidence.

I didn't have anything to worry about, other than the possibility of them finding some cheesy notes I was writing to a girl I liked. I guess my biggest fear would have been going to get some books and finding the cops hanging around the locker, passing the notes among themselves and laughing, and maybe the principal calling an assembly to read them aloud to the entire student body. (There's a high school teen crush movie scene in there somewhere, I'm sure.)

I'll also remember high school as the time when I realized that money is relative. If you're at the mall with friends and one of them is buying a pair of shoes but comes up two dollars short, you're happy to help them make up the difference. However, if you're eating in the school cafeteria, where you could get a healthy lunch consisting of a Dr. Pepper and a bag of Funyuns for $1.50, someone asking to borrow two dollars was a preposterous request, usually met with a much-deserved laugh in the face.

I went to high school in the mid to late 1980s so this was the time period in which most of the girls wore their bangs high, sticking straight up, a virtual wall of hair and hair-spray. The good news is that Britney Spears wasn't around yet so there was no chance of idolizing an eccentric blonde female pop star with a questionable private life. Well, other than Madonna.

Many of the ones I hung out with were, for a while anyway, trying to pull off the Don Johnson *Miami Vice* look—Ray-Ban sunglasses (or at least cheap knock-offs) and extremely macho pastel colored clothing. Like the girls, we had our own hair fixation: slicked back or spiked up, with several pounds of gel, creating a type of hairstyle that is best described as "crunchy." I eventually abandoned this effort and thought it would be more "original" if I tried to be like Sting. I already had the blond spiked hair, so why not? That's the way I see those years. I realize there were many other groups of people and they had different styles, but they're not easy to notice when you're always looking in the mirror. And, perspective and selective memory being what they are, others will surely remember those years differently. If you don't believe that, I would respond by quoting the lyrics from The Replacements' 1989 song "I'll Be You." But it would cost too much to get the rights to republish those lyrics here.

Speaking of music, it turns out that our senior class song was "Good Times Bad Times" by Led Zeppelin. I had to ask around for this information. This was something else I had blocked out, and with good reason. First, it wasn't a very timely song; it was released in 1969, twenty years before our graduation. Second, I have no idea what any of that song's lyrics have to do with high school.

Maybe I'm being too critical (Who, me?) but I think a better song would have been Howard Jones's "Things Can Only Get Better," even if that wasn't true. Especially since it contains this powerful message: "Whoa whoa whoa oh oh oh whoa oh oh." Or something like that, anyway.

I'll also remember all the times I was told that I daydreamed too much. "Daydreaming" is pejorative for "thinking," and very few teachers wanted any of that going on in the classroom. Much of that "daydreaming" led to quite a bit of writing, which I never shared with anyone. I was told on many occasions that because I was looking out the window or writing in a notebook that had nothing to do with the class, I was wasting time.

I now know they were wrong. It was the beginning of a discovery: I wanted to write. Whether I did it well was beside the point. It was the one thing that made me happy; the one thing I wanted to do; the one thing I was meant to do. And that discovery is really what I'll remember about high school.

ABOUT THE AUTHOR

Jeff Tompkins is from Raleigh, N.C., but now lives in Charleston, S.C., where he does *not* enjoy boating or golfing or anything like that.

You can follow his blog at jefftompkins.blogspot.com.

His next book, a novel set in 1980s suburban America, will be available in the fall of 2011.

Also by Jeff Tompkins

49 MIX TAPES

a novel

available in paperback and e-book
DECEMBER 2011

Made in the USA
Lexington, KY
29 August 2013